1A

READING
EXPLORER

THIRD EDITION

NANCY DOUGLAS

DAVID BOHLKE

NATIONAL GEOGRAPHIC
LEARNING

Australia · Brazil · Mexico · Singapore · United Kingdom · United States

NATIONAL GEOGRAPHIC

L E A R N I N G

National Geographic Learning,
a Cengage Company

Reading Explorer Split 1A
Third Edition

Nancy Douglas and David Bohlke

Publisher: Andrew Robinson

Executive Editor: Sean Bermingham

Associate Development Editor: Yvonne Tan

Director of Global Marketing: Ian Martin

Heads of Regional Marketing:

Charlotte Ellis (Europe, Middle East and Africa)

Kiel Hamm (Asia)

Irina Pereyra (Latin America)

Product Marketing Manager: Tracy Bailie

Senior Production Controller: Tan Jin Hock

Associate Media Researcher: Jeffrey Millies

Art Director: Brenda Carmichael

Operations Support: Hayley Chwazik-Gee

Manufacturing Planner: Mary Beth Hennebury

Composition: MPS North America LLC

Split 1A with Online Workbook:
ISBN-13: 978-0-357-12348-5

Split 1A:
ISBN-13: 978-0-357-12346-1

National Geographic Learning
20 Channel Center Street
Boston, MA 02210
USA

Locate your local office at **international.cengage.com/region**

Visit National Geographic Learning online at **ELTNGL.com**
Visit our corporate website at **www.cengage.com**

Printed in China
Print Number: 01 Print Year: 2019

CONTENTS

SCOPE AND SEQUENCE

UNIT	THEME	READING	VIDEO
1	Amazing Animals	**A:** The Incredible Dolphin **B:** Master of Disguise	A Chameleon's Colors
2	Travel and Adventure	**A:** The Trip of a Lifetime **B:** Adventure Islands	Exploring Laponia
3	The Power of Music	**A:** Move to the Music **B:** A Musical Boost	The Mozart Effect
4	Into Space	**A:** Life Beyond Earth? **B:** Living in Space	The Red Planet
5	City Life	**A:** Global Cities **B:** A Taste of Two Cities	New York Skyscraper
6	Backyard Discoveries	**A:** In One Cubic Foot **B:** What's in Your Neighborhood?	BioBlitz

READING SKILL	VOCABULARY BUILDING	CRITICAL THINKING
A: Skimming for Gist **B:** Identifying Main Ideas in Paragraphs	**A:** Suffixes *-ance* and *-ence* **B:** Word forms of *survive*	**A:** Identifying Ideas **B:** Comparing; Reflecting
A: Understanding Maps **B:** Scanning for Key Details	**A:** Words acting as nouns and verbs **B:** Collocations with *original*	**A:** Interpreting Visual Information **B:** Reflecting
A: Identifying Supporting Details **B:** Identifying Supporting Reasons (1)	**A:** Collocations with *control* **B:** Suffix *-ion*	**A:** Reflecting **B:** Relating to Personal Experience; Evaluating Methods
A: Summarizing: Using a Concept Map **B:** Identifying Supporting Reasons (2)	**A:** Suffix *-ful* **B:** Collocations with *environment*	**A:** Speculating **B:** Reflecting; Ranking Tasks
A: Understanding Charts and Graphs **B:** Summarizing: Using a T-chart (1)	**A:** Prefix *inter-* **B:** Suffix *-ation*	**A:** Ranking Cities **B:** Relating; Evaluating Pros and Cons
A: Understanding Sequence (1)—Processes **B:** Understanding Sequence (2)—Instructions or Directions	**A:** Phrasal verbs with *break* **B:** Collocations with *take*	**A:** Applying Ideas **B:** Analyzing Information; Applying Ideas

READING EXPLORER brings the world to your classroom.

With *Reading Explorer* you learn about real people and places, experience the world, and explore topics that matter.

What you'll see in the Third Edition:

Real-world stories give you a better understanding of the world and your place in it.

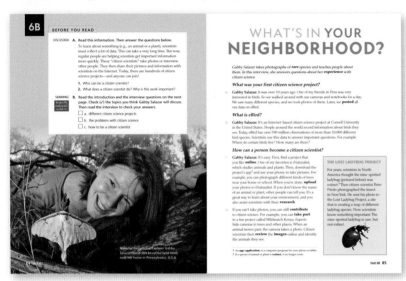

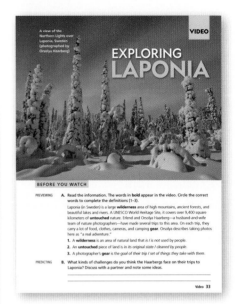

National Geographic Videos expand on the unit topic and give you a chance to apply your language skills.

Reading Skill and **Reading Comprehension** sections provide the tools you need to become an effective reader.

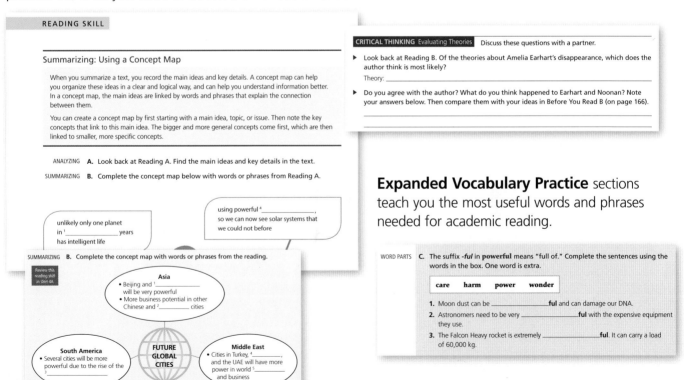

Expanded Vocabulary Practice sections teach you the most useful words and phrases needed for academic reading.

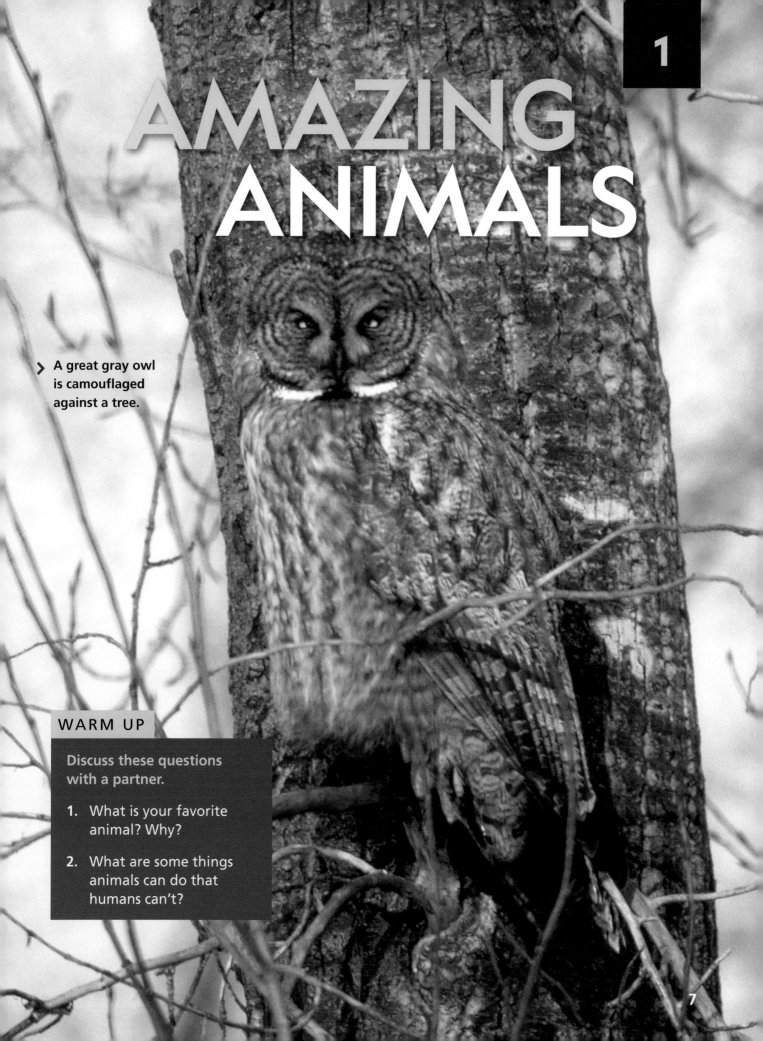

AMAZING
ANIMALS

1

> **A great gray owl is camouflaged against a tree.**

Discuss these questions with a partner.

1. What is your favorite animal? Why?

2. What are some things animals can do that humans can't?

7

BEFORE YOU READ

LABELING

A. Look at the photo. Match each description (1–4) with the correct part of the dolphin.

1. Dolphins sleep by resting one half of their **brain** at a time.

2. A dolphin's **tail** doesn't have any bones.

3. Dolphins "hear" through a special bone in their lower **jaw**.

4. The bones inside a dolphin's **flippers** look like the bones inside your arm and hand.

SKIMMING

B. Look at the reading title and headings. What is the reading about? Circle a, b, or c. Then read the passage to check your answer.

a. types of dolphins

b. things dolphins do

c. what dolphins eat

> A spotted dolphin swims in the clear waters of the Caribbean.

THE INCREDIBLE DOLPHIN

A Many people say dolphins are **intelligent**. They seem to be able to think, understand, and learn things quickly. But are they as **smart** as humans, or are they more like cats and dogs? Dolphins use their brains quite differently from the way people do. But scientists say dolphins and humans are **alike** in some ways. How?

Communication

B Like humans, every dolphin has its own "name." The name is a **special** whistle.[1] Each dolphin chooses a whistle for itself, usually by its first birthday. Dolphins are like people in other ways, too. They "talk" to each other about a lot of things—such as their age, their feelings, and possible danger. They also use a **system** of sounds and body language to **communicate**. Understanding dolphin conversation is not easy for humans. No one "speaks dolphin" yet, but some scientists are trying to learn.

Play

C Dolphins live in groups called *pods*, and they often join other dolphins from different pods to play games and have fun—just like people. Sometimes they chase other dolphins carrying objects (e.g., seaweed) and throw these objects back and forth. Scientists believe playing together is something only intelligent animals do.

Teamwork

D Dolphins and humans are similar in another way: They both make plans for getting things they want. In the seas of southern Brazil, for example, dolphins use an intelligent **method** to get food. When there are fish near a boat, dolphins signal[2] to the fishermen to put their nets in the water. With the dolphins' help, the men can catch a lot of fish. Why do dolphins **assist** the men? There is an **advantage** for the dolphins: They get to eat some of the fish that escape from the net.

---

1 A **whistle** is a high-pitched sound made by blowing air through a hole.
2 If you **signal** to someone, you make an action or a sound to tell them something.

A. Choose the best answer for each question.

MAIN IDEA

1. What does the reading NOT mention?

   a. how dolphins communicate with each other
   b. how dolphins move quickly through the water
   c. how dolphins play games and have fun

INFERENCE

2. The author mentions cats and dogs in paragraph A to show that _____.

   a. cats and dogs are very intelligent
   b. there are different levels of intelligence
   c. scientists have studied the brains of cats and dogs

DETAIL

3. Where does a dolphin get its "name"?

   a. It gets it from its mother.
   b. It gets it from scientists.
   c. It chooses it for itself.

DETAIL

4. Which sentence about dolphin language is true?

   a. Dolphins "talk" to each other about many things.
   b. Dolphin conversation is easy for humans to understand.
   c. Dolphins can't understand dolphins from other pods.

DETAIL

5. Why do dolphins sometimes help fishermen?

   a. Dolphins are kind animals.
   b. The dolphins can get food that way.
   c. The fishermen ask the dolphins for help.

CATEGORIZING

B. According to the reading passage, what do these dolphin behaviors (a–f) demonstrate? Add them to the chart.

   a. using body language
   b. chasing each other
   c. whistling
   d. joining other pods for games
   e. helping fishermen catch fish
   f. throwing seaweed back and forth

Communication	Play	Teamwork
a c	b, d, f	e

A bottlenose dolphin in the
Bay of Islands, New Zealand

Skimming for Gist

The **gist** of a passage is what the text is mainly about. When you want to get the gist of a passage, don't read every word. Skim the text quickly to find out what it is mostly about. Look at the title and any headings, photos, and captions. Another strategy is to read the first sentence of each paragraph.

SKIMMING

A. Skim Reading A again. What is the main idea of the passage? Circle a, b, or c.

a. We can learn a lot from the way dolphins communicate, play, and work together.
b. The dolphin is the most intelligent sea animal in the world.
c. Dolphins are intelligent and—in some ways—are like humans.

SKIMMING

B. Skim this short passage and answer the questions (1–2) below. Then read the passage again and check your answers.

The albatross is one of the world's largest flying birds. It also has the largest wings of any bird—up to 3.4 meters from tip to tip. These giant birds use their wings to ride the ocean winds. They can fly for hours without rest, or even without moving their wings. Some may even be able to sleep while flying.

Most albatrosses spend nearly all their time in the air. In fact, they only return to land to breed.[1] A parent albatross might fly thousands of kilometers to find food for its young. In its lifetime, an albatross can fly a total of more than six million kilometers.

A wandering albatross

1 When animals **breed**, they have babies.

1. What is the above passage mainly about?
   a. where albatrosses live
   b. albatross flying behavior
   c. albatross intelligence

2. What could be a title for this passage?
   a. Riding the Ocean Winds
   b. Catching Fish
   c. The Smartest Bird

CRITICAL THINKING Identifying Ideas

▶ Reading A mentions three similarities between dolphins and humans. What are they?

communication   play   Teamwork

▶ Can you think of other ways to tell if an animal is intelligent? Discuss with a partner and note some ideas.

Dogs, They can understand human's language

DEFINITIONS **A.** Read the paragraph below and match each word in **red** with its definition (1–5).

There are a few ways to test how **smart** animals are. One **method** is to test memory. Scientists in Japan showed a group of college students and a group of five-year-old chimps the numbers 1 to 9 in different places on a computer screen. The test was to see if the groups could remember the position of the numbers in the correct order. Each time, the chimps were faster than the students. Why? Were the chimps **special** in some way? Did someone **assist** them? No, but the chimps probably had an important **advantage**: They were young. As both humans and animals get older, their memory gets worse.

1. _method_ : a way of doing something
2. _assist_ : to help
3. _smart_ : clever
4. _special_ : better or more important than others
5. _advantage_ : something that helps you succeed

COMPLETION **B.** Complete the information with the words from the box.

alike	communicate	feelings	intelligent	system

⌄ **A Sumatran orangutan**

Orangutans and humans are ¹ _alike_ in some ways. Both are very ² _intelligent_ animals. For example, to stay dry when it rains, orangutans take leaves from trees and use them like umbrellas. These apes don't have a complex[1] language ³ _system_ like humans do. But today, some orangutans are learning basic sign language to express their thoughts and ⁴ _feeling_. New research also suggests that orangutans can ⁵ _communicate_ about the past, just like humans.

1 If something is **complex**, it is complicated or made up of many parts.

WORD PARTS **C.** Some nouns use the suffixes *-ance* and *-ence*. Use the noun form of these words to complete the sentences. Add the correct suffix to each word.

assist	different	intelligent

1. What is the _differences_ between a dolphin and a porpoise?
2. The fact that apes use tools shows they have great _intelligence_.
3. Whales will often give _assistance_ to other whales that are in danger.

BEFORE YOU READ

DEFINITIONS **A.** Read the caption below. Then circle the correct words to complete these definitions.

    1. If you **disguise** yourself, you change how you look so others *know* / *don't know* who you are.

    2. A **predator** is an animal that eats *other animals* / *plants*.

    3. If two animals **look like** each other, they look *different* / *the same*.

SKIMMING **B.** Look at the picture on page 15 and read the caption and labels. Then skim the passage and complete the sentence below. Read the passage to check your answer.

Review this reading skill in Unit 1A

Most of the passage explains *why* / *how* octopuses disguise themselves.

< Octopuses **disguise** themselves so **predators** (e.g., dolphins or sharks) don't see them. Here, the octopus **looks like** the coral nearby.

MASTER OF DISGUISE

A   Octopuses are famous for their round bodies, big eyes, and eight arms. There are many different types of octopuses, but all are alike in one way: They are masters[1] of disguise. Octopuses can change their **appearance** in less than a second to look like rocks, plants, or even other animals. How do they do this?

B   An octopus can disguise itself in three ways. One is by using color. An octopus's skin has special cells[2] called *chromatophores*. These cells are filled with yellow, brown, and red pigment.[3] When an octopus moves its **muscles** a certain way, the cells become large and **produce** colorful spots and other **patterns** on its skin. Chromatophores can also reflect light. In blue light, for example, an octopus's skin will look blue. In white light, its skin will look white. With these cells, an octopus can produce many different skin colors and patterns.

C   An octopus can also change its skin texture.[4] When the octopus moves its muscles, its skin can go from smooth to spiky. It might then look like a plant, or coral. Another way an octopus disguises itself is by changing its **shape**. Some, for example, roll their bodies into balls so they look like rocks. One type of octopus can change its form to look like other sea **creatures**—especially dangerous ones, such as sea snakes.

D   Why are octopuses so good at disguising themselves? They have to be. The ocean is not a safe place for them. Because they have no bones in their bodies, octopuses are like large pieces of meat. Many predators want to eat them—and they can eat them whole. To **survive**, octopuses have **developed** the amazing **ability** to change their appearance very quickly in order to **hide** from predators.

---

1 A **master** is very good at doing something.
2 A **cell** is the smallest living part of an animal or plant. Most animals have billions of cells in their bodies.
3 **Pigment** is a substance that gives something color. For example, green pigment makes most plants look green.
4 **Texture** is how something looks and feels (e.g., soft, smooth, spiky).

ALL MUSCLE, NO BONES

An octopus's body has many muscles. This makes it strong and fast. Octopuses also have no bones, so they can change their shape very quickly.

An octopus brain holds only one-third of the animal's neurons (nerve cells). It handles functions such as decision-making, learning, and memory.

An octopus has three hearts: one large central heart and two smaller ones on either side.

About two-thirds of an octopus's neurons are in its arms. These neurons control the arm movements.

Octopuses can change their appearance to match their surroundings. Once the brain gives a signal, the octopus's muscles move in a certain way, changing its skin from smooth to spiky and producing colorful spots or stripes on its skin.

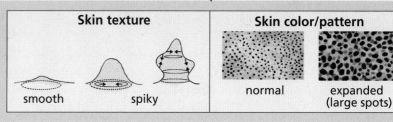

Skin texture

smooth   spiky

Skin color/pattern

normal   expanded (large spots)

A. Choose the best answer for each question.

GIST   **1.** What would be the best alternative title for this passage?

    a. The Mind of an Octopus
    b. How an Octopus Hides
    c. Octopus Numbers on the Rise

DETAIL   **2.** Which of these sentences is NOT true?

    a. Chromatophores are light-reflecting cells.
    b. Chromatophores can change in size.
    c. Chromatophores produce an animal's skin texture.

INFERENCE   **3.** In red light, an octopus probably appears _____ .

    a. red
    b. blue
    c. white

INFERENCE   **4.** In paragraph C, the author suggests that some corals _____ .

    a. can change their color
    b. can roll themselves into balls
    c. have spiky outer surfaces

REFERENCE   **5.** What does *they* refer to in paragraph D, line 4?

    a. octopuses
    b. bones
    c. predators

MATCHING   **B. Look at the list of ways octopuses disguise themselves (a–c) and the statements (1–5). Match each statement with the method of disguise. Write a, b, or c.**

    a. color   b. skin texture   c. shape

    ___a___ **1.** by producing spots on their skin
    ___c___ **2.** by appearing to be sea snakes
    ___c___ **3.** by rolling their bodies into balls
    ___a___ **4.** by reflecting light
    ___b___ **5.** by making their skin spiky

> **A Pacific red octopus shows its suckers.**

Identifying Main Ideas in Paragraphs

A paragraph usually has one main idea and some details that support it. Paragraphs often include a topic sentence that describes the main idea. Usually—but not always—a topic sentence is at or near the start of the paragraph, or at the end. One way to find the main idea quickly is to read the sentences at the beginning and end of the paragraph. A paragraph's heading (if it has one) can also give a clue to its main idea.

MAIN IDEA

A. Read the paragraph below. Which sentence gives the main idea? Circle a, b, or c.

Is it a stick? Or is it an insect? It's a stick insect—an insect that looks like a stick. The stick insect is an example of an animal that uses color, texture, and shape to disguise itself. It lives—and can easily hide—among the leaves and twigs of plants. Most stick insects are either brown or green. The smallest types are just over a centimeter long. The largest is about 33 centimeters, making it one of the world's longest insects.

∧ **A Malayan giant stick insect**

a. The stick insect is an example of an animal that uses color, texture, and shape to disguise itself.

b. It lives—and can easily hide—among the leaves and twigs of plants.

c. The largest is about 33 centimeters, making it one of the world's longest insects.

MAIN IDEA

B. Look back at Reading B. Match each paragraph with its main idea (a–d).

1. Paragraph A •   • a. An octopus can change its shape and skin texture.

2. Paragraph B •   • b. Octopuses can change how they look very quickly.

3. Paragraph C •   • c. An octopus can change its skin color.

4. Paragraph D •   • d. Octopuses disguise themselves for their own protection.

CRITICAL THINKING Comparing   Which animal do you think is smarter—the dolphin or the octopus? Why? Note your ideas and discuss with a partner.

_____

_____

_____

VOCABULARY PRACTICE

COMPLETION **A.** Complete the paragraph with words from the box.

ability	appearance	hide	patterns	produce

Reef squid—like their relatives, octopuses—have an amazing
¹____ability____: They can quickly change their physical
²__appearance__ in order to ³____hide____ from
predators. They also use this skill to send messages; they can
even ⁴__produce__ two messages at the same time!
For example, a male reef squid swimming near a female squid
can create colorful, attractive ⁵__patterns__ on the side
of its body closest to the female. On the other side, it shows
black and white lines that tell other male squid to stay away.

▽ **A bigfin reef squid**

WORDS IN CONTEXT **B.** Complete each sentence with the correct answer (a or b).

1. A **creature** refers to any living _animal (b)_ .
   a. plant   b. animal
2. A circle has a _round (a)_ **shape**.
   a. round   b. square
3. If you **survive** a dangerous situation, you _live (a) (b)_
   through it.
   a. live   b. don't live
4. The **muscles** in the human body control how we _move (b)_ .
   a. think   b. move
5. If you **develop** a skill or ability, it becomes _better or stronger (a)_ .
   a. better or stronger   b. worse or weaker

WORD FORMS **C.** The verb **survive** can be made into a noun by adding the suffixes **-or** or **-al**.
Complete the sentences with the correct words from the box.

survive	survivor	survival

1. The ___survival___ of whales is connected to the health of the ocean.
2. These plants cannot ___survive___ in very cold conditions.
3. The plane crash had only one ___survivor___ .

> **A chameleon balances on a thin branch.**

A CHAMELEON'S COLORS

BEFORE YOU WATCH

PREVIEWING **A.** Read the extracts from the video. Then complete the definitions of the words or phrases in **bold**. Circle the correct words.

"Chameleons can change color to **attract** other chameleons or to **warn** them to go away."

"To catch food, a chameleon hides in the trees until an insect walks by. Then it **shoots out** its tongue …"

1. If you want to **attract** something, you want it to *come to you / go away*.

2. When you **warn** someone about something, you tell them that something *good / bad* may happen.

3. When something **shoots out**, it moves very *quickly / slowly*.

QUIZ **B.** Read the sentences below and guess if they are correct. Circle **T** (true) or **F** (false).

1. The main reason chameleons change color is to hide from predators.	**T**	**F**
2. A chameleon's tongue is very long.	**T**	**F**
3. Chameleons are in trouble because they are being hunted by other animals.	**T**	**F**

GIST **A.** Watch the video. Check your answers in Before You Watch B.

MULTIPLE CHOICE **B.** Watch the video again. Choose the correct answer for each question.

1. According to the video, where do many different types of chameleons live?

a. Malta

b. Madagascar

2. What is one reason given in the video for chameleons' color changes?

a. to show that they want some food

b. to show that they are scared

3. Why do chameleons rock back and forth?

a. to stay safe from predators

b. to get ready to attack other animals

4. The video uses a model of a bow and arrow to _____ .

a. show how difficult it is for a predator to attack a chameleon

b. explain how a chameleon can stick out its tongue very fast

CRITICAL THINKING Reflecting   If you were a scientist studying animals, what animal would you study? What would you like to find out about this animal? Note some ideas and share your answers with a partner.

_____

_____

_____

VOCABULARY REVIEW

Do you remember the meanings of these words? Check (✓) the ones you know. Look back at the unit and review any words you're not sure of.

Reading A

☐ advantage ☐ alike ☐ assist* ☐ communicate* ☐ feelings

☐ intelligent* ☐ method* ☐ smart ☐ special ☐ system

Reading B

☐ ability ☐ appearance ☐ creature ☐ develop ☐ hide

☐ muscle ☐ pattern ☐ produce ☐ shape ☐ survive*

* Academic Word List

TRAVEL AND ADVENTURE

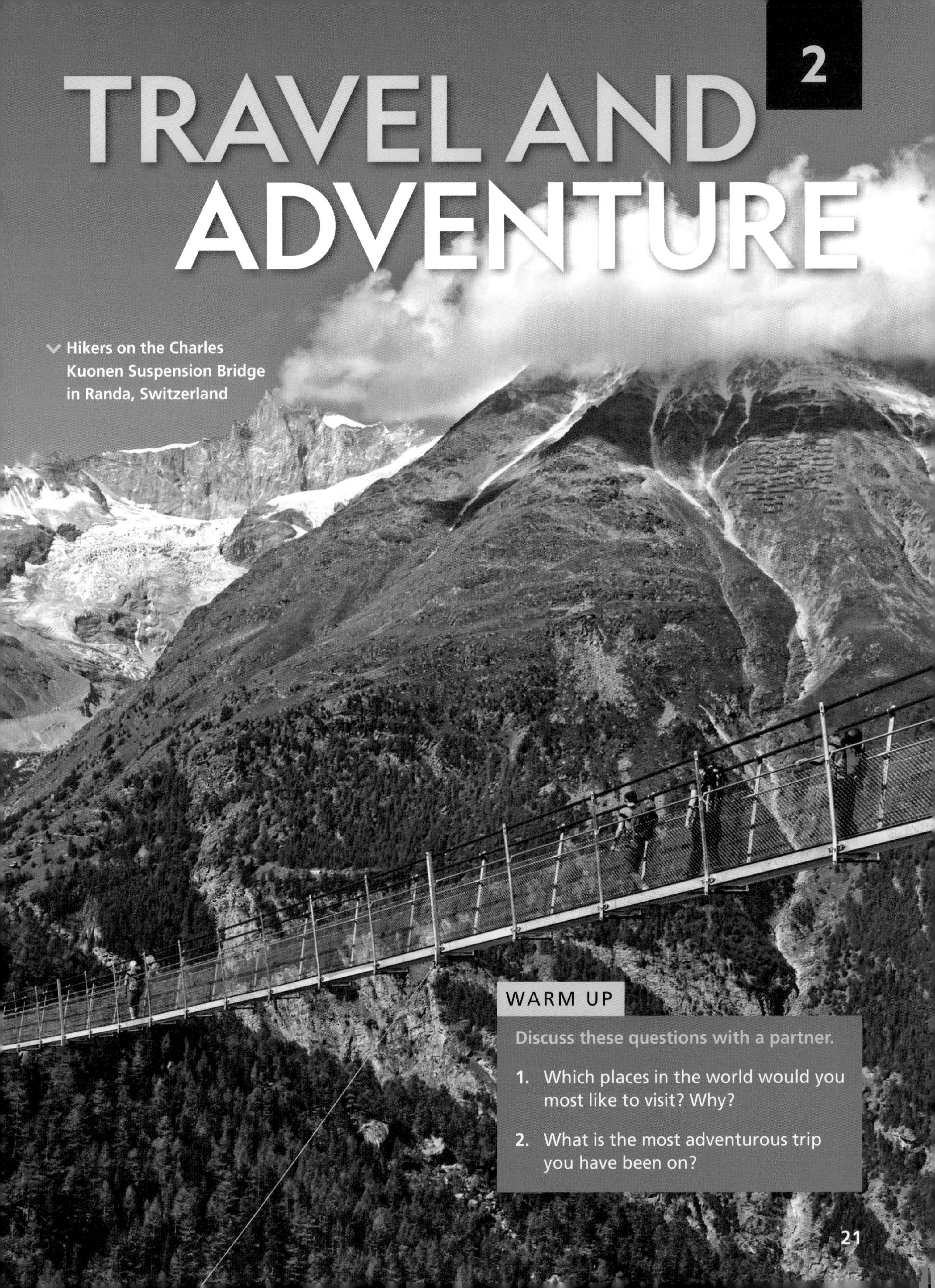

⌄ Hikers on the Charles
Kuonen Suspension Bridge
in Randa, Switzerland

WARM UP

Discuss these questions with a partner.

1. Which places in the world would you most like to visit? Why?

2. What is the most adventurous trip you have been on?

21

START
Prudhoe Bay, AK

CYCLING THE AMERICAS

In 2005, Gregg Bleakney and his friend Brooks Allen began an amazing two-year cycling adventure.

Route ⌒

Total distance: 30,500 kilometers

▦ mountains

San Francisco, CA

Mexico City, Mexico

Panama City, Panama

BEFORE YOU READ

SCANNING **A.** Use the map and the information above to answer these questions.

1. Where did the two friends travel from and to? How did they travel?

2. How far did they travel? How long did the trip take?

DISCUSSION **B.** Why do you think they wanted to make this trip? Discuss with a partner.

La Paz, Bolivia

FINISH — Ushuaia, Argentina

THE TRIP OF A LIFETIME

A Many people dream of going on a great travel adventure. Most of us keep dreaming; others make it happen.

B Gregg Bleakney's dream was to travel the Americas from top to bottom. He got the idea after he finished a 1,600-kilometer bike ride. Gregg's friend Brooks Allen was also a cyclist. The two friends talked and decided on their **goal**: They would travel from Alaska to Argentina—by bike.

C To pay for the **journey**, Gregg and Brooks worked and saved money for years. In 2005, after four years of planning, they set off. Once they were on the road, they often camped outdoors or stayed in hostels.[1] In many places along their **route**, local people opened their homes to the two friends and gave them food.

---

1 A **hostel** is a cheap place to stay when traveling.

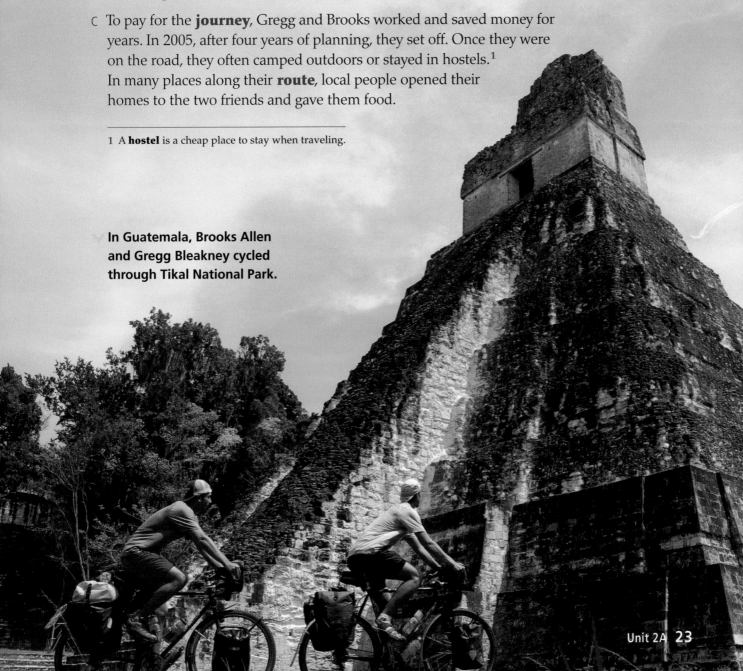

In Guatemala, Brooks Allen and Gregg Bleakney cycled through Tikal National Park.

Lessons from the Road

D During their trip, Gregg and Brooks cycled through deserts, rain forests, and mountains. They visited **modern** cities and explored **ancient** ruins,[2] such as Tikal in Guatemala. In many places, they met other cyclists from all over the world.

E In May 2007—two years, 12 countries, and over 30,500 km later—Gregg eventually reached Ushuaia, Argentina, at the southern tip of South America. (Halfway through the trip, Brooks had to stop. He returned to the United States and Gregg continued without him.)

F Gregg and Brooks kept a **record** of their adventures in an online blog. The trip taught both men a lot about traveling. Here is some of Gregg's **advice**.

- **Travel light.** The less baggage you have, the less you'll **worry** about.
- **Be flexible.** Don't plan everything. You'll be more **relaxed** and happy, even when there are **challenges** along the way.
- **Be polite.** As one traveler told Gregg, "Always remember that nobody wants to fight, cheat, or rob[3] a nice guy."

---

2 The **ruins** of something are the parts that remain after it is damaged or weakened.
3 If someone **robs** you, they take money or property from you.

⌄ **Many Antarctic cruises start from the port of Ushuaia in Argentina.**

A. Choose the best answer for each question.

GIST **1.** What could be another title for the reading?

a. Cycling from Alaska to Argentina
b. Things to Do and See in America
c. Argentina: The Land of Adventure ✓

DETAIL **2.** Which sentence about the trip is NOT true?

a. To pay for the trip, Gregg and Brooks saved money and traveled cheaply on the road.
b. During their trip, Gregg and Brooks met cyclists from all around the world.
d. Only Brooks made the complete trip from Alaska to Argentina.

VOCABULARY **3.** In paragraph F, what does *baggage* mean?

a. things you take on a trip
b. places you visit on a trip
c. reasons for going on a trip

PARAPHRASE **4.** What does Gregg mean by *Be flexible* in paragraph F?

a. Be careful when you travel.
b. Be ready to change easily.
c. Plan the details of your trip.

INFERENCE **5.** Which statement would Gregg most likely agree with?

a. When you travel, only stay in hotels or with people you know.
b. Bring a lot of things on your trip so you don't have to buy anything.
c. When abroad, learn how to say "thank you" in the local language.

▲ **In Prudhoe Bay, Alaska, the sun does not set from mid-May through mid-July.**

MAIN IDEA **B.** Match each paragraph with its main idea.

Review this reading skill in Unit 1B

1. Paragraph B •   • a. what the cyclists saw on their trip
2. Paragraph C •   • b. what the cyclists learned from their trip
3. Paragraph D •   • c. a dream of cycling through the Americas
4. Paragraph E •   • d. how the cyclists paid for their trip
5. Paragraph F •   • e. when and where the cycling trip ended

Understanding Maps

Like other visuals, maps can help you better understand a text. Most maps have a **title**, a **scale** (to show distance), a **key** or **legend** (a guide of symbols or colors used), and a **source** (where the information comes from). A map may also include a **compass** (to show where north is).

LABELING **A.** Look at the map below. Label the parts of the map with these features (1–5).

1. key　　　**2.** source　　　**3.** scale　　　**4.** title　　　**5.** compass

THE ANCIENT MAYA EMPIRE

During its golden age (A.D. 250 to 900), the Maya Empire included what is now southeastern Mexico, Guatemala, Belize, and the western areas of Honduras and El Salvador.

COMPLETION **B.** Use information from the map above to complete these sentences. Circle the correct words.

1. The ancient city of Teotihuacan in Mexico *was / was not* part of the Maya Empire.

2. The distance from Teotihuacan to Tikal is *less / greater* than 400 kilometers.

3. Tikal is located in *northern / southern* Guatemala. It is close to the border with *Honduras / Belize.*

CRITICAL THINKING Interpreting Visual Information　Look back at the map on page 22. Which parts of the journey do you think were the most challenging for the cyclists? Why? Discuss with a partner and note your ideas.

WORDS IN CONTEXT

A. Complete each sentence with the correct answer (a or b).

1. If something is **ancient**, it is very _____.
   a. expensive   (b.) old

2. _____ is an example of a **modern** invention.
   (a.) The cell phone   b. Paper

3. A **record** of an event will help you _____ it.
   a. change   (b.) remember

4. If something is a **challenge**, it is _____ to do.
   (a.) difficult   b. easy

COMPLETION

B. Complete the information using words from the box.

advice   goals   journey   relax   route   worry

Every year, many people make mistakes when they go hiking. Here's some ¹ _advice_ that can help you stay safe.

Before you start your ² _journey_ , leave a map showing the ³ _route_ that you are planning to take. If something goes wrong (for example, if you get lost), you should "S.T.O.P." This means:

- **S**top: try to ⁴ _relax_ and stay calm.
- **T**hink about your situation.
- **O**bserve: look around and notice where you are.
- **P**lan what to do next: set one or two simple ⁵ _goals_ for yourself.

It's also important to stay on clearly marked trails. Don't ⁶ _worry_ —someone will eventually find you.

› **Hikers in the Austrian Tyrol**

WORD USAGE

C. Some words such as **record** can be either a noun (pronounced "**re**cord") or a verb (pronounced "re**cord**"). Complete the sentences with the correct words from the box. Then circle the stressed syllable in each word.

address   object   record

1. We found a strange _object_ among the ruins.
2. Once I've found somewhere to live, I'll send you my new _address_ .
3. You should _record_ your travels in a travel diary.

Land diving on Pentecost Island, Vanuatu

BEFORE YOU READ

DISCUSSION **A.** Look at the photo. Then answer the questions below with a partner.

    1. What do you think is happening in the photo?

    2. What is the most dangerous sport or activity you have tried?

PREDICTING **B.** Look at the reading title and headings. What do you think these activities have in common? Check your ideas as you read.

ADVENTURE ISLANDS

A Vanuatu is a **nation** of small islands in the South Pacific. It is one of the smallest countries in the world. But for those interested in adventure and sport, there is a lot to do. Some of the best swimming, snorkeling, and sea kayaking can be found here. Vanuatu's islands also offer visitors two of the most exciting— and dangerous—activities in the world: volcano surfing and land diving.

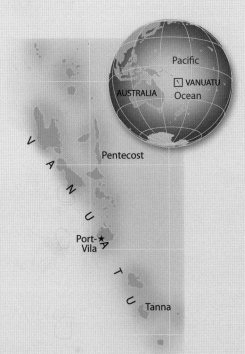

Volcano Surfing

B On Tanna Island, Mount Yasur rises 300 meters into the sky. Yasur is one of Vanuatu's few **active** volcanoes. It erupts[1] **almost** every day, sometimes several times a day. For **centuries**, both locals and tourists have climbed this mountain to visit the top. Recently, people have also started climbing Yasur to surf the volcano. In some ways, volcano surfing is like surfing in the sea, but in other ways, it's very different. A volcano surfer's goal is to **escape** the erupting volcano—without being **hit** by flying rocks! It's fast, fun, and dangerous—the perfect extreme sport.[2]

Land Diving

C Most people are **familiar** with bungee jumping. But did you know that bungee jumping started on Pentecost Island in Vanuatu almost 15 centuries ago? The **original** activity—called land diving—is part of a religious ceremony.[3] A man **ties** two tree vines[4] around his ankles. He then climbs a wooden tower around 20 to 30 meters high, crosses his arms, and jumps headfirst. The goal is to touch the earth with the top of his head—without breaking the vines or hitting the ground hard. Every spring, local boys and men still perform this amazing test of **bravery**. Women are not allowed to dive, but they support the divers by dancing and singing at the bottom of the tower. Many tourists come to the island every year to watch this ancient tradition.

---

1 When a volcano **erupts**, it throws out hot rock called lava.

2 An **extreme sport** is a sport that is dangerous and exciting, such as skydiving or bungee jumping.

3 A **ceremony** is a formal event, such as a wedding.

4 A **vine** is a plant that grows up or over things.

A. Choose the best answer for each question.

PURPOSE

1. What is the purpose of this reading?

    a. to compare Vanuatu with other islands in the South Pacific
    b. to explain what volcano surfing and land diving are
    c. to talk about the world's best volcano surfer and land diver

MAIN IDEA

2. How are volcano surfing and land diving similar?

    a. They are both ancient sports.
    b. Anyone can do them.
    c. They are both extreme activities.

REFERENCE

3. In paragraph A, what does *those* refer to?

    a. people
    b. countries
    c. islands

DETAIL

4. Which sentence is true about Mount Yasur?

    a. It is no longer active.
    b. People have been climbing it for a long time.
    c. It is on Pentecost Island.

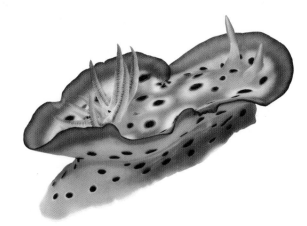

∧ **Vanuatu is also a popular destination for scuba divers. Underwater creatures there include extremely colorful sea slugs like this one.**

DETAIL

5. Which sentence is true about land diving?

    a. It was first called "bungee jumping."
    b. It is less popular today than in the past.
    c. It is a traditional activity in Vanuatu.

EVALUATING STATEMENTS

B. Are the following statements true or false according to the reading passage, or is the information not given? Circle T (true), F (false), or NG (not given).

1. Vanuatu has more than one active volcano.	T F NG
2. Volcano surfing came to Vanuatu from another country.	T F NG
3. More people get hurt volcano surfing than land diving.	T F NG
4. Both men and women can do land diving.	T F NG
5. The land diving ceremony is a popular tourist attraction.	T F NG

Scanning for Key Details

When you read, you often want to find specific details in the text. Before you read, you first need to decide what to look for (e.g., a person's name, a place, or a number). Once you know what to look for, scan the text quickly to find that information.

ANALYZING **A.** Read the questions. What kind of answer will you need to scan for? Circle a, b, or c. (Do not answer the questions yet.)

1. Where can you surf in cold water?

   (a.) a place　　　　　b. a number　　　　　c. a date

2. How high are the highest waves on the "silver dragon"?

   a. an example　　　　(b.) a number　　　　c. a reason

3. Why is surfing possible in so many places?

   (a.) a reason　　　　b. a place　　　　c. an example

4. What other hobby is popular among surfers?

   a. a place　　　　b. a reason　　　　(c.) an activity

SCANNING **B.** Now scan the text below and write answers to the questions above.

1. _Antarctica_
2. _10 meters_
3. _needs two things_
4. _skateboarding_

When you think of surfing, you probably think of Hawaii, Australia, or Brazil. But surfers don't need warm weather, or even an ocean. For example, some surfers ride the waves in the icy cold waters of Antarctica. Other surfers head to China's Qiantang River to surf the "silver dragon." Twice a year, the waves on the Qiantang can reach a height of 10 meters.

Surfing is possible in all these places because a surfer only needs two things: a wave and a board. There is always a risk, so surfers need to be strong swimmers. They also need good balance and an ability to think and move quickly. This is why skateboarding is a common hobby among surfers.

CRITICAL THINKING Reflecting　Imagine a tourist wants to try an extreme sport or activity in your country. Where would you suggest they go? What should they do? Note some ideas and share them with a partner.

VOCABULARY PRACTICE

COMPLETION **A.** Circle the correct words to complete the information below.

If you lead an ¹**almost** / **active** lifestyle and want to
learn an extreme water sport, consider whitewater
kayaking. Many people head to Chile every year to
kayak along the many rivers and rapids¹ that the
²**bravery** / **nation** is known for. The United States also
has many popular kayaking spots, such as the Great Falls
of the Potomac River. The falls lie ³**almost** / **familiar**
entirely within the state of Maryland.

Whitewater kayaking is very dangerous. So why do
people do it? For some, it is a test of ⁴**centuries** /
bravery. For others, it makes them feel alive.

1 **Rapids** are a section of a river where the water moves very fast, often over rocks.

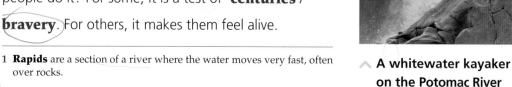

∧ **A whitewater kayaker
on the Potomac River**

DEFINITIONS **B.** Complete the definitions using words from the box.
One word is extra.

| active century escape familiar hit original tie |

1. If you _____hit_____ something, you touch it with a lot of force.
2. Something that is ____original____ is the very first of its kind.
3. A(n) ____century____ is a period of a hundred years.
4. If you are ____familiar____ with something, you know or understand it well.
5. If you ____tie____ two things together, you join them using rope or string.
6. If you ____escape____ from something, you run away from it.

COLLOCATIONS **C.** The nouns in the box are often used with the word **original**. Complete the
sentences with the correct nouns from the box.

| idea   owner   song |

1. The land was returned to its original ____owner____.
2. The students came up with a very original ____idea____ for how to solve
the problem.
3. We wrote and performed an original ____song____ for the music competition.

A view of the Northern Lights over Laponia, Sweden (photographed by Orsolya Haarberg)

EXPLORING LAPONIA

BEFORE YOU WATCH

PREVIEWING
A. Read the information. The words in **bold** appear in the video. Circle the correct words to complete the definitions (1–3).

Laponia (in Sweden) is a large **wilderness** area of high mountains, ancient forests, and beautiful lakes and rivers. A UNESCO World Heritage Site, it covers over 9,400 square kilometers of **untouched** nature. Erlend and Orsolya Haarberg—a husband-and-wife team of nature photographers—have made several trips to this area. On each trip, they carry a lot of food, clothes, cameras, and camping **gear**. Orsolya describes taking photos here as "a real adventure."

1. A **wilderness** is an area of natural land that *is / is not* used by people.

2. An **untouched** piece of land is *in its original state / cleaned by people*.

3. A photographer's **gear** is the *goal of their trip / set of things they take with them*.

PREDICTING
B. What kinds of challenges do you think the Haarbergs face on their trips to Laponia? Discuss with a partner and note some ideas.

_____

_____

GIST   **A.** Watch the video. Were any of your predictions in Before You Watch B mentioned in the video? What other challenges are mentioned? Note them below.

_____

_____

SHORT ANSWER   **B.** Watch the video again. Write a short answer for each question.

1. Is it easier to explore Laponia in winter or in summer? Why?

_____

2. What are some types of food the Haarbergs carry with them?

_____

3. What happened to Orsolya on one trip?

_____

CRITICAL THINKING Reflecting   Think about the activities or adventures you have learned about in this unit. Which ones would you want to try? Which ones would you not want to try? Note your answers and reasons, and share them with a partner.

_____

_____

_____

VOCABULARY REVIEW

Do you remember the meanings of these words? Check (✓) the ones you know. Look back at the unit and review any words you're not sure of.

Reading A

☐ advice ☐ ancient ☐ challenge* ☐ goal* ☐ journey

☐ modern ☐ record ☐ relaxed* ☐ route* ☐ worry

Reading B

☐ active ☐ almost ☐ bravery ☐ century ☐ escape

☐ familiar ☐ hit ☐ nation ☐ original ☐ tie

* Academic Word List

THE POWER OF MUSIC

3

Hip-hop group Migos performs at the 2018 Coachella Valley Music and Arts Festival in California.

WARM UP

Discuss these questions with a partner.

1. What is your favorite kind of music? Who is your favorite singer or band?

2. How important is music in your life? Give reasons and examples to support your answer.

35

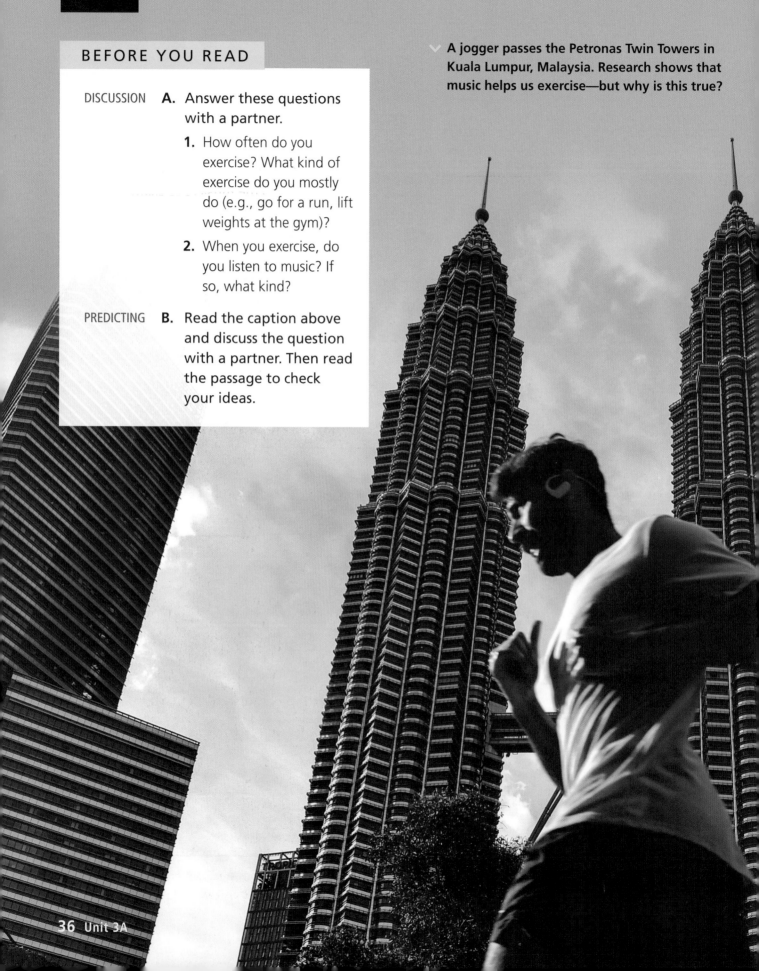

3A

DISCUSSION **A.** Answer these questions with a partner.

1. How often do you exercise? What kind of exercise do you mostly do (e.g., go for a run, lift weights at the gym)?

2. When you exercise, do you listen to music? If so, what kind?

PREDICTING **B.** Read the caption above and discuss the question with a partner. Then read the passage to check your ideas.

A jogger passes the Petronas Twin Towers in Kuala Lumpur, Malaysia. Research shows that music helps us exercise—but why is this true?

MOVE
TO THE MUSIC

A Music helps us exercise—but why does it have this effect? Experts say there are two main reasons. The first is simple: Music **distracts** us. When we listen to a song we like, our brain **pays attention** to the music. For example, after we exercise for 20 minutes, our body might be tired. But we may not feel this immediately because we are listening to music. So we exercise a little longer.

B Music also motivates[1] us. When we hear dance music, for example, we naturally start to move to the **beat**. An upbeat[2] song also puts us in a good **mood**, so we feel happier. This gives us **energy** and helps us exercise longer. Music with a quick and **steady** beat is good for exercising. But the music shouldn't be *too* fast, says sports psychologist Dr. Costas Karageorghis. Generally, songs in the **range** of 120–140 beats per minute (BPM) are the best.

---

1 If something **motivates** you, it makes you want to do something.
2 An **upbeat** song is one that is lively and cheerful.

Beats per minute (BPM) is a term for measuring the speed of a piece of music. The higher the BPM, the faster the song. Here's a short playlist of popular workout music with the BPM for each song.

- "Lose Yourself" – Eminem (86 BPM)
- "Stronger (What Doesn't Kill You)" – Kelly Clarkson (116 BPM)
- "Idol" – BTS (126 BPM)
- "I Gotta Feeling" – The Black Eyed Peas (128 BPM)
- "On the Floor" – Jennifer Lopez featuring Pitbull (130 BPM)
- "Locked Out of Heaven" – Bruno Mars (144 BPM)
- "Mr. Brightside" – The Killers (148 BPM)

ᐱ **Bruno Mars is a Grammy Award-winning singer, songwriter, and producer.**

C A new study by cognitive scientist[3] Tom Fritz suggests this is only part of the explanation, however. In an experiment, Fritz put 61 people in small groups. They all then exercised twice. One time, each group worked out while listening to music for six minutes. Another time, they exercised for six minutes on special Jymmin machines. The name Jymmin is a combination of "jammin'" and "gym." Using these machines, each group made music as they moved. At the end, 53 of the 61 people said the same thing: They felt less tired when they exercised on the Jymmin machines. When we exercise and *make* music—especially with other people—working out **seems** to be easier.

D How does Fritz explain this? Maybe people did better on the Jymmin machines because they had more **control**, he says. People created the beat. They could make it go faster or slower. Also, the activity was **social**. Each group was making music together and having fun. Fritz believes that Jymmin exercise may have other advantages, too. He wants to find out if it can help with more serious conditions. For example, it may even be a good way to treat depression.[4]

---

3 A **cognitive scientist** is a person who studies the mind and how people think and learn.

4 **Depression** is a medical condition in which a person feels very sad and is often unable to live in a normal way.

▾ **A group of people exercise using Jymmin machines.**

READING COMPREHENSION

A. Choose the best answer for each question.

GIST

1. What is the reading mainly about?
- (a.) the effect of music on exercise
- b. good songs for a workout music playlist
- c. how Jymmin machines work

VOCABULARY

2. In paragraph A, what does the word *immediately* mean?
- a. completely
- b. sometimes
- (c.) right away

DETAIL

3. According to the passage, which of these songs is at the ideal speed for exercising?
- a. "Lose Yourself" – Eminem
- (b.) "I Gotta Feeling" – The Black Eyed Peas
- c. "Locked Out of Heaven" – Bruno Mars

MAIN IDEA

4. Paragraphs C and D focus on the advantages of _____ while exercising.
- a. listening to music
- b. watching music videos
- (c.) creating music

INFERENCE

5. Which of these can we definitely say about Jymmin machines?
- a. People exercised better using the machines because they had more control.
- (b.) People using the machines could make the music go faster or slower.
- c. The machines are useful in treating depression.

SUMMARIZING

B. Complete the summary below using words from the box. One word is extra.

control	depression	distracts	make	motivate	range	tired

One reason listening to music helps us exercise is that it ¹_____distracts_____ us.

When we listen to a song we enjoy, our mind pays attention to the music, so we don't

feel ²_____tired_____. Another reason music helps us exercise is that it can

³_____motivate_____ us to keep exercising.

A recent study shows that people exercise better when they use special machines

that allow them to ⁴_____make_____ music while exercising with other people.

They felt this gave them more ⁵_____control_____. Also, it made exercising a fun,

social activity. In the future, these machines could even be used to help people who

suffer from ⁶_____depression_____.

Identifying Supporting Details

The main ideas of a text are usually supported by details. These give more information about the main idea, and can include examples, facts, or reasons.

MATCHING **A.** The sentences below (1–3) relate to Reading A. Match each sentence with the type of supporting detail it contains (a, b, or c).

a. example   b. fact   c. reason

_b_ **1.** Dr. Tom Fritz works at the Max Planck Institute for Human Cognitive and Brain Sciences.

_a_ **2.** Jymmin exercise may help even serious conditions such as depression.

_c_ **3.** Music helps us exercise because it distracts us.

SUPPORTING DETAILS **B.** Read this paragraph and underline the main idea. Then use supporting details in the paragraph to answer the questions (1–3).

Generally, songs with 120–140 beats per minute (BPM) are the best for exercising. This is because most people want to get their heart rate up to this level during a workout. Songs in this range include Lady Gaga's "The Edge of Glory" (128 BPM) and "Push It" (130 BPM) by Salt-N-Pepa. Listening to songs like these can increase your endurance[1] by up to 15 percent. A slower song like Adele's "Make You Feel My Love" (72 BPM) is more likely to make you want to relax, or even take a nap.

1 **Endurance** is the ability to keep doing something difficult, unpleasant, or painful for a long time.

1. Why are songs in the 120–140 BPM range good for exercising?

_____

2. Who sang the song "The Edge of Glory"?

_____

▲ **In 2015, Adele's *25* broke the iTunes record for fastest-selling album.**

3. What is an example of a song that is not suitable for exercising?

_____

CRITICAL THINKING Reflecting When you exercise, do you prefer listening to songs in English or in your own language? Note your answer and reasons below. Include examples of songs. Then discuss with a partner.

_____

_____

VOCABULARY PRACTICE

COMPLETION **A.** Complete the paragraph with words from the box. One word is used twice.

beat	energy	range	seems	steady

Much of the research done on music and exercise focuses on what the ideal BPM
¹____*range*____ is for running. But it also ²____*seems*____ from recent
studies that having a predictable, ³____*steady*____ rhythm is important. Generally,
music with sudden changes in the ⁴____*beat*____, like free-form jazz, is less
suitable. Why? If the music speed changes while we run, we tend to adjust our
movements to match the ⁵____*beat*____. Each time we change our steps to
move faster or slower, we lose ⁶____*energy*____.

COMPLETION **B.** Complete the sentences using words or phrases from the box.

control	distract	pay attention	mood	social

∧ **Pharrell's "Happy"
was the best-selling
song of 2014 in the
United States.**

1. Music can sometimes ____*distract*____ you from
   your work.
2. Many people say that listening to the song "Happy" by
   Pharrell Williams puts them in a good ____*mood*____.
3. If you want to have better ____*control*____ of your
   singing voice, you should do more vocal exercises.
4. Most schools organize ____*social*____ events like
   dances and concerts for the students.
5. Orchestra musicians must ____*pay attention*____ to the
   conductor during a performance.

COLLOCATIONS **C.** The prepositions in the box are often used with the word **control**. Complete
the definitions below with the correct prepositions.

in	out of	under

1. If you are ____*in*____ control of a company, you have the power to make
   important decisions about the way it is run.
2. If a situation is ____*under*____ control, it is being dealt with successfully and is
   unlikely to cause any problems.
3. If something is ____*out of*____ control, it cannot be dealt with successfully.

For most activities, we use several functions, or abilities, controlled by different parts of our brain.

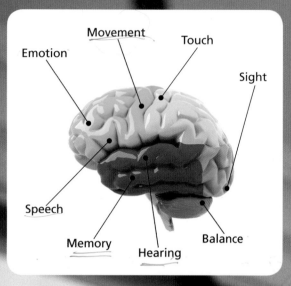

Emotion
Movement
Touch
Sight
Speech
Memory
Hearing
Balance

BEFORE YOU READ

DISCUSSION

A. Discuss the following questions with a partner.

1. Look at the brain diagram and the caption above. Which function(s) do you use when you sing? Play an instrument? Listen to music?

2. In what ways do you think music and language are similar?

PREDICTING

guess

B. Look at the reading title. What do you think *boost* means?

a. a change for the better

b. a problem

c. a system

Check your answer as you read the passage.

ᴬMUSICAL BOOST

A   Is there a **connection** between music and language? According to recent studies, the answer is yes: Music boosts **certain** language abilities in the brain. Here are two examples.

Music and Hearing

B   A study from Northwestern University shows that playing a musical instrument can **improve** a person's hearing ability. As a part of the study, two groups of people listened to a person talking in a noisy room. The people in the first group were musicians, while those in the second group had no musical training. The musicians were able to hear the talking person more clearly.

C   Musicians hear better, says study leader Nina Kraus, because they learn to pay attention to certain sounds. Think about violinists in an orchestra. When the violinists play with the group, they hear their own instrument and many others, too. But the violinists must listen closely to what they are playing, and **ignore** the other sounds. In this way, musicians are able to **concentrate** on certain sounds, even in a room with lots of noise.

Music and Speech

D   Gottfried Schlaug, a doctor at Harvard Medical School, works with stroke[1] patients. Because of their illness, these people cannot say their names, addresses, or other information **normally**. However, they can still sing. Dr. Schlaug was surprised to find that singing words helped his patients to eventually speak. Why does this work? Schlaug isn't sure. Music seems to activate[2] different parts of the brain, including the **damaged** parts. This somehow helps patients use those parts of the brain again.

Understanding the Results

E   Music improves concentration, memory, listening **skills**, and our **overall** language abilities. It can even help sick people get better. Playing an instrument or singing, says Nina Kraus, can help us do better in school and keep our brains **sharp** as we get older. Music, therefore, is not only enjoyable; it's also good for us in many other ways.

---

1   A **stroke** is an illness of the brain. It can make a person unable to move one side of their body.
2   If you **activate** something, you make it start working.

A. Choose the best answer for each question.

GIST

1. What could be another title for the "Music and Hearing" section?

  a. Trained to Listen
  b. How to Be a Musician
  c. Playing in an Orchestra

DETAIL

2. What two groups did Nina Kraus study?

  a. noisy people and quiet people
  b. musicians and nonmusicians
  c. violinists and other musicians

REFERENCE

3. What does *they* refer to in paragraph C, line 3?

  a. orchestra musicians
  b. instruments
  c. violinists

DETAIL

4. What is true about Nina Kraus and Gottfried Schlaug?

  a. They both work at Harvard Medical School.
  b. They both play an instrument in an orchestra.
  c. They are both interested in how music and the brain are connected.

DETAIL

5. How does Gottfried Schlaug help stroke patients speak?

  a. by playing music for them
  b. by getting them to sing words
  c. by teaching them to play instruments

Studies have suggested that playing classical music to babies may make them smarter.

EVALUATING STATEMENTS

B. Are the following statements true or false according to the reading passage, or is the information not given? Circle T (true), F (false), or NG (not given).

	T	F	NG
1. In the Northwestern University study, the nonmusicians could hear better.	T	F	NG
2. Nina Kraus can play the violin very well.	T	F	NG
3. People who speak well can learn to play an instrument quickly.	T	F	NG
4. Gottfried Schlaug isn't sure why music helps stroke patients.	T	F	NG
5. Studies show that listening to music helps people sleep better.	T	F	NG
6. Nina Kraus believes that singing lessons can help students get better grades in school.	T	F	NG

5284 *make n edu*
n tor.

Identifying Supporting Reasons (1)

Reasons are a type of supporting detail (see Unit 3A Reading Skill). A text may contain <u>one or more</u> <u>reasons</u> why something happens. Identifying *why* things happen helps you better understand the relationship between things in the text. The reason may appear before or after the action or effect. Words or phrases that signal reasons include *because* (*of*), *since*, and *due to*. In the following examples, the reason is underlined.

Musicians hear better because <u>they learn to pay attention to certain sounds</u>.

Singing words may help stroke patients since <u>this activates a different part of the brain</u>.

Because of <u>this need to concentrate</u>, musicians hear many sounds more clearly.

NOTICING **A. Read the passage below. Circle the words or phrases that signal reasons.**

How has Western music reached almost every corner of the world? Researchers believe Western music is popular because of its ability to express emotions across cultures.

Researcher Tom Fritz played parts of 42 Western songs to members of the Mafa, an ethnic group in Cameroon. Since he wanted to include a variety of Western music types, Fritz played classical, rock, pop, and jazz. He asked the group members to point to pictures of people's faces to show the emotion the music expressed.

Cameroon

The Mafa were able to identify the emotions correctly. This was probably due to the fact that the rhythms and melodies of Western music are similar to those of basic human speech. So some part of the way we understand Western music is shared by everyone, regardless of our own cultures.

SUPPORTING REASONS **B. Answer these questions with the supporting reasons from the passage.**

1. Why do researchers believe Western music is popular?

Because of its ability to express emotions across cultures

2. Why did Tom Fritz play classical, rock, pop, and jazz music?

Since he wanted to include a varity of western music

3. Why were the Mafa able to identify the emotions correctly?

The rhythms and melodies of western music are similar to those of basic human speech

CRITICAL THINKING Relating to Personal Experience   Does listening to music help you study or concentrate? If so, what kinds of music help you? What other factors might help you concentrate better? Note your answers and share them with a partner.

Yes I do, PoP likes Adel, stable

VOCABULARY PRACTICE

WORDS IN CONTEXT

A. Complete each sentence with the correct answer (a or b).

1. If you **ignore** something, you ___a___ it.
   a. don't pay attention to   b. focus on

2. A **certain** sound refers to ___a___ type of sound.
   a. only one   b. any

3. If you **concentrate**, you ___a___ .
   a. think very hard   b. don't think at all

4. Two examples of **skills** are ___b___ .
   a. food and drink   b. cooking and sewing

5. A person's **overall** abilities means their abilities ___b___ .
   a. related to a single skill   b. as a whole

COMPLETION

B. Complete the paragraph with words from the box.

connection	damaged	improved	normally	sharp

In his book *Musicophilia*, brain scientist Dr. Oliver Sacks looked at the ¹_connection_ between music and the brain. He wrote about how music ²_improved_ the lives of musicians, hospital patients, and ordinary people. Dr. Sacks also shared the experiences of different people. He gave an example of a man whose brain was ³_damaged_ by a lightning strike, which—strangely—left him wishing to become a musician at age 42. Another interesting example was of a man whose memory ⁴_normally_ lasted only seven seconds, except when he listened to music. When this happened, his mind became very ⁵_sharp_, with a near-perfect memory.

Dr. Oliver Sacks
(1933–2015)

WORD FORMS

C. We can add *-ion* to some verbs to form nouns (e.g., **connect** + *-ion* = **connection**). Complete the sentences below using the verbs in the box. One verb is extra.

act	connect	discuss	react

1. Scientists still have a lot to learn about the _connect_**ion** between language and music.

2. The new Taylor Swift song has received mixed _react_**ions**.

3. The issue of music education in schools is a major topic of _discuss_**ion** these days.

Classical musicians perform at a restaurant in Moscow.

THE MOZART EFFECT

BEFORE YOU WATCH

PREVIEWING **A.** Read the information. The words and phrases in **bold** appear in the video. Match these words and phrases with their definitions (1–3).

Many people enjoy listening to classical music (e.g., the music of Mozart). There have been claims that listening to classical music makes you smarter and raises **IQ**. This theory is called the "Mozart Effect." To test this theory, University of Virginia psychologist Dr. Jim Coan carried out an **experiment**. He gave people some word puzzles and asked them if they could **figure out** the answers, both before and after listening to classical music. What do you think the results showed? Can classical music make people smarter? Dr. Coan's findings may surprise you.

1. _____ : to understand or solve something

2. _____ : a number that represents a person's level of intelligence

3. _____ : a scientific test done in order to learn something

QUIZ **B.** In the video, Dr. Coan uses word puzzles to test people's IQ (e.g., "7 DOTW" stands for "7 days of the week"). Can you figure out what these puzzles mean? Discuss with a partner.

- 12 MOTY
- 7 WOTW
- 24 HIAD
- 18 HOAGC

GIST **A.** Watch the video. Write the answers to the puzzles below. Were your answers in Before You Watch B correct?

- 12 MOTY = _____
- 7 WOTW = _____
- 24 HIAD = _____
- 18 HOAGC = _____

MULTIPLE CHOICE **B.** Watch the video again. Choose the correct answer for each question.

1. Most of the people in the experiment _____ after listening to classical music.

  a. did better   b. showed no change

2. What other kind of music (besides classical music) did the people in the video listen to?

  a. hip-hop music   b. rock music

3. Which of these statements summarizes Dr. Coan's findings?

  a. Classical music is more effective than other kinds of music at improving people's focus and problem-solving abilities.

  b. Any kind of music can improve people's reasoning abilities, as long as they enjoy listening to it.

CRITICAL THINKING Evaluating Methods   Discuss these questions with a partner.

▶ Can you think of any weaknesses in Dr. Coan's methods? What are some other possible reasons for people's improved performance in his experiment?

▶ Can you think of a better way to test the Mozart Effect? Plan your own experiment.

VOCABULARY REVIEW

Do you remember the meanings of these words? Check (✓) the ones you know. Look back at the unit and review any words you're not sure of.

Reading A

☐ beat	☐ control	☐ distract	☐ energy*	☐ mood
☐ pay attention	☐ range*	☐ seem	☐ social	☐ steady

Reading B

☐ certain	☐ concentrate*	☐ connection	☐ damaged	☐ ignore*
☐ improve	☐ normally*	☐ overall*	☐ sharp	☐ skill

* Academic Word List

4

INTO SPACE

Astronaut David A. Wolf takes a spacewalk outside the International Space Station.

WARM UP

Discuss these questions with a partner.

1. What movies or TV shows about space have you seen? Describe them.

2. Do you think there is life in outer space? Why or why not?

The Kepler Space Telescope was sent off into space
in 2009. Named after Johannes Kepler—a German
astronomer from the 17th century—it discovered
over 2,600 **planets** during its lifetime. As a result,
scientists now believe that there are probably more
planets than stars in our **galaxy**.

BEFORE YOU READ

DEFINITIONS

A. Read the caption above and match
the words in **bold** with their
definitions (1–4).

1. Mars, Jupiter, and Earth are all
_____Planets_____.

2. A(n) _____galaxy_____ is a very
large group of stars, gas, and dust.

3. A(n) _____Telescope_____ makes
distant objects appear closer.

4. A(n) _____astronomer_____ studies
stars and other objects in space.

SKIMMING

Review this
reading skill
in Unit 1A

B. Skim the passage quickly. What do
Shostak and Barnett think?

a. We might soon communicate with
beings from space.

b. We will probably never find
intelligent life outside Earth.

c. We have probably already
contacted beings from space.

Check your answer as you read.

LIFE BEYOND EARTH?

A Is there intelligent life on other planets besides Earth? For years, scientists weren't sure. Today, this is changing. Seth Shostak and Alexandra Barnett are astronomers. They believe intelligent life **exists** elsewhere in the universe. They also think we will soon **contact** these beings.

B Why do these astronomers think intelligent life exists on other planets? The first reason is time. Scientists believe the universe is about 12 billion years old. According to Shostak and Barnett, this is too long a period for only one planet in the **whole** universe to develop intelligent life. The second reason is size—the universe is huge. **Tools** such as the Hubble Telescope have shown that "there are at least 100 billion … galaxies," says Shostak. And our galaxy—the Milky Way— has at least 100 billion stars. Some planets that **circle** these stars might be similar to Earth.

The **universe** is all of space—all the stars, planets, and other objects.

A person or a living creature (e.g., an animal) is a **being**.

Looking for Intelligent Life

C   Until recently, it was difficult to **search** for signs of intelligent life in the universe. But now, **powerful** telescopes **allow** scientists to **identify** many more small planets—the size of Mars or Earth—in other solar systems.[3] If these planets are similar to Earth and are close enough to a star, they might have intelligent life.

Making Contact

D   Have beings from outer space already visited Earth? Probably not, says Shostak. The **distance** between planets is too great. Despite this, intelligent beings might eventually contact us using other methods, such as radio signals[4] or flashes of light.[5] In fact, they could be trying to communicate with us now, but we may not have the right tools to receive their messages. This is changing, however, says Shostak. He predicts that we will make contact with other life forms in our universe within the next 20 years.

---

3 The **solar system** is made up of the sun and all the planets that orbit around it.

4 A **radio signal** is a way of sending information using radio waves.

5 A **flash of light** is a sudden, short burst of bright light.

❮ Scientists are hoping to build spaceships that could reach the closest stars.

A. Choose the best answer for each question.

PURPOSE

1. What is the main purpose of this reading?

   a. to discuss how life probably started on Earth
   b. to explain why we might find intelligent life outside of Earth
   c. to describe what life on other planets might look like

DETAIL

2. Which possible reason for the existence of intelligent life is NOT mentioned?

   a. Some planets that circle stars might be similar to Earth.
   b. The universe is too old to have just one planet with intelligent life.
   c. Some other planets in the Milky Way have water.

DETAIL

3. According to the reading passage, why was it difficult to search for signs of intelligent life in the past?

   a. Telescopes weren't powerful enough.
   b. The distance between planets was too great.
   c. There were too few trained astronomers.

VOCABULARY

4. What does *life forms* in the last sentence of the passage mean?

   a. messages   b. beings   c. planets

DETAIL

5. Why does Shostak think we will make contact with intelligent life within the next 20 years?

   a. We will have better technology to receive their messages.
   b. Bigger telescopes will identify more planets like Earth.
   c. Intelligent life will finally receive messages that we send to them.

SHORT ANSWER

B. Write short answers for these questions. Use information from the reading passage.

1. What tool has been used to discover billions of galaxies?

   Power telescope

2. Does Shostak think that beings from other planets have visited Earth?

   Probably not

3. Besides radio signals, what else could other life forms use to contact us?

   flashes of light

NASA has found what looks like a large moon orbiting a planet outside our solar system. This could be the first known alien moon.

Summarizing: Using a Concept Map

When you summarize a text, you record the main ideas and key details. A concept map can help you organize these ideas in a clear and logical way, and can help you understand information better. In a concept map, the main ideas are linked by words and phrases that explain the connection between them.

You can create a concept map by first starting with a main idea, topic, or issue. Then note the key concepts that link to this main idea. The bigger and more general concepts come first, which are then linked to smaller, more specific concepts.

ANALYZING **A.** Look back at Reading A. Find the main ideas and key details in the text.

SUMMARIZING **B.** Complete the concept map below with words or phrases from Reading A.

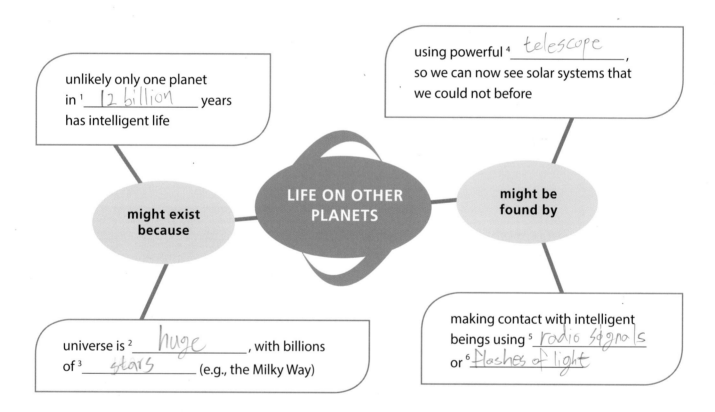

using powerful ⁴ _telescope_ , so we can now see solar systems that we could not before

unlikely only one planet in ¹ _12 billion_ years has intelligent life

LIFE ON OTHER PLANETS

might exist because

might be found by

universe is ² _huge_ , with billions of ³ _stars_ (e.g., the Milky Way)

making contact with intelligent beings using ⁵ _radio signals_ or ⁶ _flashes of light_

CRITICAL THINKING Speculating Imagine a space station receives a radio signal from another planet confirming intelligent life there. What do you think would happen next? Discuss with a partner and note your ideas.

_____

_____

VOCABULARY PRACTICE

COMPLETION **A.** Circle the correct words to complete the paragraph below.

Is there life on other planets? Scientists use different methods to try to answer this question. Some use very [1]**powerful** / **whole** radio telescopes. They hope to receive messages from intelligent life on distant planets. Other scientists only [2]**search** / **contact** for life in our solar system. But they aren't looking for intelligent life—they want to [3]**circle** / **identify** any possible life forms. To do this, they test whether conditions on a planet would [4]**allow** / **contact** any kind of life to [5]**exist** / **search**.

WORDS IN CONTEXT **B.** Complete each sentence with the correct answer (a or b).

1. We measure **distance** in _____.
   a. kilometers (km)
   b. kilograms (kg)

2. Some examples of **tools** are _____.
   a. monkeys and dolphins
   b. cell phones and laptops

3. If you **contact** someone, you _____ them.
   a. meet or communicate with
   b. research and write about

4. If you have lived in a place your **whole** life, you have lived there _____ of your life.
   a. some
   b. all

5. If a spaceship **circles** a planet, it _____ the planet.
   a. goes around
   b. lands on

▲ **The SpaceX Falcon Heavy rocket lifted off on February 6, 2018.**

WORD PARTS **C.** The suffix *-ful* in **powerful** means "full of." Complete the sentences using the words in the box. One word is extra.

care	harm	power	wonder

1. Moon dust can be _____harm_____**ful** and can damage our DNA.
2. Astronomers need to be very _____care_____**ful** with the expensive equipment they use.
3. The Falcon Heavy rocket is extremely _____power_____**ful**. It can carry a load of 60,000 kg.

BEFORE YOU READ

COMPLETION **A.** Read these definitions. Then complete the paragraph below with the correct form of the words in **bold**.

astronaut: a person who travels into space

colony: a place under the control of another place, usually another country

establish: to make or start something (e.g., a system or an organization)

rocket: a vehicle used to travel to space

Robert Zubrin is a(n) ¹_____ scientist; he designs spaceships. He thinks we should send a group of ²_____ into space, but not just to visit. Zubrin wants to ³_____ a human ⁴_____ on Mars. He wants to change the planet into a new place for humans to live.

PREDICTING **B.** Read the sentence below. Circle your answer and complete the sentence. Then compare your ideas with those in the passage.

Sending humans into space to live *is / is not* a good idea because

_____

_____.

▲ **This is what a colony on Mars might look like in the future.**

LIVING IN SPACE

A Stephen Hawking, one of the world's most famous scientists, believed that to survive, humans will one day have to move into space. "Once we spread out into space and establish **independent** colonies, our future should be safe," he said.

B Today, the United States, Europe, Russia, China, and Japan are all planning to send astronauts back to Earth's closest **neighbor**: the moon. Some of these countries want to create space stations there within the next 10 years. These stations will prepare humans to visit and later live on Mars or other Earthlike planets.

C Robert Zubrin, a rocket scientist, thinks humans should colonize space. He wants to start with Mars. Why? He thinks sending people to Mars will allow us to learn a lot of things—for example, the ability of humans to live in a very different **environment**. Eventually, we could create new human societies on other planets. In addition, any **advances** we make in the fields of science, technology, **medicine**, and health will **benefit** people here on Earth.

D SpaceX is a company that builds rockets. Its founder and CEO, Elon Musk, also believes we should colonize Mars. He doesn't want to send just "one little **mission**," though. His long-term goal is to put one million people on the planet in case something bad happens to us here on Earth.

E Not everyone thinks sending humans into space is a smart idea. Many say it's too expensive. Also, most space trips are not short. A one-way trip to Mars, for example, would take at least six months. People traveling this kind of distance could face many health problems. In addition, these first people would find life extremely difficult in space. On the moon's **surface**, for example, the sun's rays[1] are very dangerous. People would have to stay indoors most of the time.

F Despite these **concerns**, sending people into space seems certain. In the future, we might see lunar[2] cities or even new human **cultures** on other planets. First stop: the moon.

---

1 The **sun's rays** are narrow beams of light from the sun.
2 **Lunar** means "related to the moon."

A. Choose the best answer for each question.

PURPOSE

1. What is the main purpose of this passage?

    a. to give reasons for and against space colonization

    b. to describe what life would be like on the moon

    c. to compare the environments of Mars and the moon

REFERENCE

2. What does *our* in Stephen Hawking's quote "our future should be safe" (paragraph A) refer to?

    a. scientists'

    b. humans'

    c. colonies'

DETAIL

3. Why are some countries planning to build lunar space stations?

    a. to learn more about the moon's surface

    b. to reduce the number of people living on Earth

    c. to prepare humans to live on other planets

DETAIL

4. Which reason for living in space is NOT mentioned?

    a. We can learn if humans can live in a very different environment from that of Earth.

    b. We can establish human societies on other planets besides Earth.

    c. We can search for signs of intelligent life elsewhere in the universe.

A Japanese food company has developed vacuum-packed ramen noodles that can be eaten easily in space.

PARAPHRASE

5. What does *First stop: the moon* mean in the last sentence?

    a. Everybody wants to visit the moon first.

    b. All spaceships to other planets have to stop at the moon first.

    c. The first human colony in space will likely be on the moon.

MAIN IDEA

Review this reading skill in Unit 1B

B. Match each paragraph with its main idea.

1. Paragraph B •

2. Paragraph C •

3. Paragraph D •

4. Paragraph E •

    • a. There are several reasons not to send humans to space.

    • b. A mission to Mars should be designed on a large scale.

    • c. Many countries are planning missions to the moon and beyond.

    • d. There are a number of reasons to travel to Mars.

Identifying Supporting Reasons (2)

A reading text will sometimes contain arguments for and against an idea. It can be useful to identify and list all the reasons for and against an idea. This can help you form your own opinion on a particular topic.

ANALYZING **A.** Look back at Reading B. Read paragraph C and recall its main idea. Then underline the reasons that support the main idea.

COMPLETION **B.** Now read paragraph E of Reading B. Complete the concept map below by writing the reasons in the boxes.

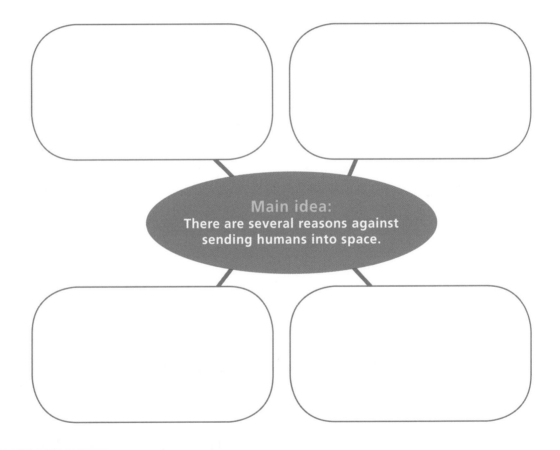

Main idea:
There are several reasons against sending humans into space.

CRITICAL THINKING Reflecting

▶ Imagine you have a chance to join a new colony on Mars. Would you go? Why or why not? Note your answer and reasons below.

_____

_____

▶ Compare your reasons above with your answers in Before You Read B (on page 56). Has Reading B changed your opinion in any way? Discuss with a partner.

VOCABULARY PRACTICE

DEFINITIONS **A.** Read the paragraph and match each word in **red** with its definition (1–5).

A **mission** to our planetary **neighbor** Mars would take at least a year—six months to get there and six months to return. This sounds like a long time. But what's more difficult than getting to Mars is actually living there. People who want to live in this **environment** would need water to survive, and they would probably have to take it with them from Earth. Recently, however, scientists found signs of a large body of liquid water under the **surface** of the planet. If confirmed, it would make people on Mars more **independent** from Earth.

1. _____ : able to live on one's own

2. _____ : the outer part of something

3. _____ : a special trip that has an aim or a goal

4. _____ : a person, country, or thing located nearby

5. _____ : the things and conditions around a person, animal, or plant

WORDS IN CONTEXT **B.** Complete each sentence with the correct answer (a or b).

1. A student of **medicine** probably wants to be a(n) _____ .

  a. doctor   b. astronaut

2. A person's **culture** includes _____ .

  a. their way of life   b. how they breathe

3. If we make **advances** in science or technology, we _____ in those areas.

  a. do worse   b. improve

4. If something **benefits** you, it _____ you.

  a. helps   b. hurts

5. A **concern** is a fact or situation that _____ you.

  a. surprises   b. worries

∧ **Water-ice clouds drift over the surface of Mars.**

COLLOCATIONS **C.** The words in the box are often used with the word **environment**. Complete the sentences with the correct words from the box.

safe	unfamiliar	work

1. "Culture shock" is a common reaction to moving to a new, _____ environment.

2. My colleagues have tried to create a friendly _____ environment.

3. Every child has the right to grow up in a(n) _____ environment.

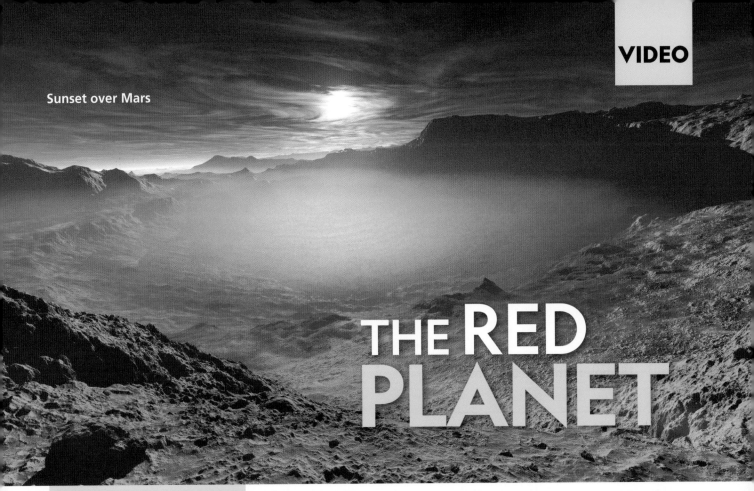

Sunset over Mars

THE RED PLANET

BEFORE YOU WATCH

PREVIEWING **A. Read the information. The words in bold appear in the video. Match these words with their definitions (1–3).**

Mars—otherwise known as "the Red Planet"—has fascinated scientists for a long time. With a diameter[1] of 6,778 km, it is about half the size of Earth. The air on Mars would kill a human quickly, and its surface is dry and **barren**. However, some scientists think life existed there in the past—and may exist again. They believe that we will all have to leave Earth one day, so they hope to **launch** manned missions to Mars and form a colony there. For these scientists, Mars might be the key to the survival of **humanity**.

---

1 The **diameter** of a round object is the length of a straight line that can be drawn across it, passing through the center.

1. _____ : all people on Earth

2. _____ : unable to produce plants or fruit

3. _____ : to send into the air or into space

QUIZ **B. Read the sentences below and guess if they are correct. Circle T (true) or F (false).**

1. Mars is more than five billion years old.	**T**	**F**
2. Mars is named after the Roman god of love.	**T**	**F**
3. Mars has the largest volcano in the solar system.	**T**	**F**
4. The volcanoes on Mars are still active.	**T**	**F**

GIST   **A.** Watch the video. Check your answers in Before You Watch B.

COMPLETION   **B.** Watch the video again. Complete this concept map.

Formed about [1]_____ billion years ago

Has water in the form of polar [6]_____ caps

The second [2]_____ planet in the solar system

Facts About Mars

Temperatures as low as [5]_____°C

Diameter similar to the width of [3]_____

Surface area similar to all of [4]_____ continents combined

CRITICAL THINKING Ranking Tasks   Imagine you are one of the first people to colonize Mars. How important would these tasks be for your colony? Rank them 1–4 (1 = most important; 4 = least important). Then compare answers with a partner and give reasons.

_____ setting up a fast communication channel with Earth

_____ developing a spacesuit that is easy to wear and move around in

_____ establishing an effective heating system to keep people's houses warm

_____ finding a way to grow fresh fruit and vegetables

VOCABULARY REVIEW

Do you remember the meanings of these words? Check (✓) the ones you know. Look back at the unit and review any words you're not sure of.

Reading A

☐ allow   ☐ circle   ☐ contact*   ☐ distance   ☐ exist

☐ identify*   ☐ powerful   ☐ search   ☐ tool   ☐ whole

Reading B

☐ advance   ☐ benefit*   ☐ concern   ☐ culture*   ☐ environment*

☐ independent   ☐ medicine   ☐ mission   ☐ neighbor   ☐ surface

* Academic Word List

5

CITY LIFE

WARM UP

Discuss these questions with a partner.

1. Why do you think so many people choose to live in cities?

2. What are some of the world's most important cities? Why are they important?

The mirrored entrance to Tokyu Plaza Omotesando Harajuku reflects the busy streets of Tokyo.

63

5A

‹ **A gargoyle on Notre-Dame Cathedral looks out over Paris.**

BEFORE YOU READ

DISCUSSION **A.** Study the graph on the next page and discuss these questions with a partner.

    1. Have you been to any of the cities listed on the graph? What were they like?

    2. How are the top four cities similar to and different from one another?

PREDICTING **B.** Which other cities do you think will become important in the future? Why? Discuss with a partner. Then check your ideas as you read the passage.

GLOBAL CITIES

A   "New York City is a star—the city of cities," wrote author John Gunther. But what makes a city great? To answer this question, the creators of the Global Cities Index looked at the following:

- **Business** – How many global companies are in the city? Does the city do a lot of **international** business?

- **People** – Does the city **attract** talented[1] people from around the world? Are the city's universities good? How many residents have college degrees?

- **Media** – Is it easy to get information from different **sources** (TV, radio, Internet)? How many residents have Internet **access**?

- **Entertainment** – Does the city have many entertainment **options**: museums, sports, music, and different types of restaurants?

- **Politics** – How many embassies[2] and international **organizations** are in the city?

1   A **talented** person has special skills and can do something well.
2   An **embassy** is a government building where officials from a foreign country work.

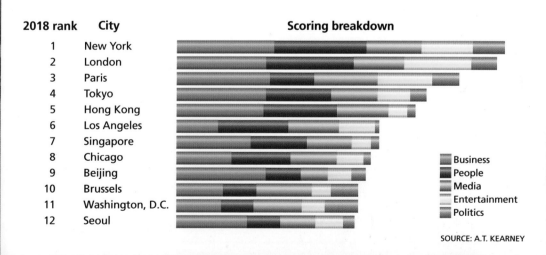

The Global Cities Index is a list of the world's most powerful and important cities. The top 12 cities in 2018 are listed here.

2018 rank	City	Scoring breakdown
1	New York	
2	London	
3	Paris	
4	Tokyo	
5	Hong Kong	
6	Los Angeles	
7	Singapore	
8	Chicago	
9	Beijing	
10	Brussels	
11	Washington, D.C.	
12	Seoul	

Business
People
Media
Entertainment
Politics

SOURCE: A.T. KEARNEY

Future Leaders

B   As the graph on the previous page shows, most cities on the Global Cities Index are strong in certain areas. Beijing's strength, for example, is business, while Los Angeles's strength is people. New York, London, and Paris are at the top because they are strong in all five areas.

C   Which cities will become more powerful in the future? Creators of the Global Cities Index **predict** the most growth in the following places:

- **Asia:** Beijing and Shanghai are both business centers and will continue to grow. In a few years, they will be as powerful as New York. Other Chinese cities such as Guangzhou and Shenzhen will also grow. Indian cities such as Mumbai and New Delhi have a lot of business **potential**, too.

- **South America:** Rio de Janeiro and São Paulo in Brazil, Buenos Aires in Argentina, and Bogotá in Colombia will become more powerful. In these cities, the middle class[3] is growing, and life for many people is improving.

- **The Middle East:** Istanbul in Turkey, Cairo in Egypt, and the cities of the United Arab Emirates (UAE) such as Dubai and Abu Dhabi will hold more power in international **politics** and business—**especially** in helping East and West work together.

D   In 10 years, the top cities on the index may be different, but one thing is certain: With over 50 percent of the world's people now living in urban areas, tomorrow's global cities will be more powerful than ever.

---

3 The **middle class** is a category of people. They earn more than the working class, but less than the upper class. It includes professionals and business people.

An evening view of central Cairo

A. Choose the best answer for each question.

GIST **1.** What is the reading mainly about?

    a. why certain global cities are important

    b. daily life in the world's fastest-growing cities

    c. Asian cities that will be important in 10 years

DETAIL **2.** What is NOT considered in the Global Cities Index?

    a. food

    b. weather

    c. education

DETAIL **3.** According to the reading, which part of the world is predicted to grow in the area of politics?

    a. Asia

    b. South America

    c. the Middle East

VOCABULARY **4.** In paragraph D, what does *urban* refer to?

    a. cities and towns

    b. the future

    c. the globe

INFERENCE **5.** Which statement would the writer probably agree with?

    a. A top global city needs to be strong in several areas.

    b. The Global Cities Index will probably list the same top cities 10 years from now.

    c. Tomorrow's global cities will probably be less powerful than today's.

SUMMARIZING **B. Complete the concept map with words or phrases from the reading.**

Review this reading skill in Unit 4A

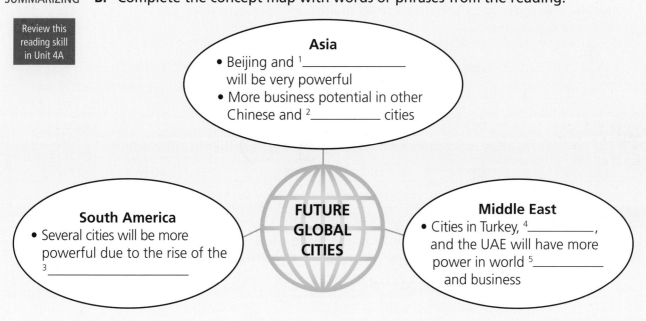

Asia
- Beijing and 1_____ will be very powerful
- More business potential in other Chinese and 2_____ cities

FUTURE GLOBAL CITIES

South America
- Several cities will be more powerful due to the rise of the 3_____

Middle East
- Cities in Turkey, 4_____, and the UAE will have more power in world 5_____ and business

Understanding Charts and Graphs

Charts and graphs may contain important details not mentioned in the text. One of the most common types of graphs is the bar graph. A bar graph uses either horizontal bars going across (the *x*-axis) or vertical bars going up (the *y*-axis) to show comparisons among categories. For example:

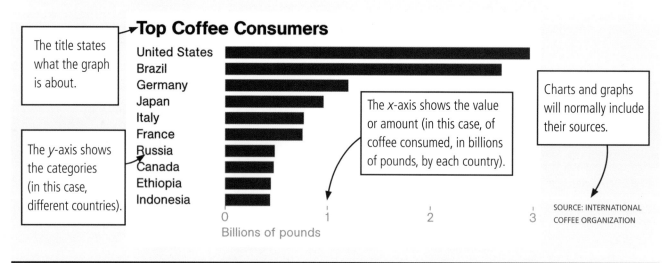

Top Coffee Consumers

The title states what the graph is about.

The *y*-axis shows the categories (in this case, different countries).

The *x*-axis shows the value or amount (in this case, of coffee consumed, in billions of pounds, by each country).

Charts and graphs will normally include their sources.

United States
Brazil
Germany
Japan
Italy
France
Russia
Canada
Ethiopia
Indonesia

0   1   2   3

Billions of pounds

SOURCE: INTERNATIONAL COFFEE ORGANIZATION

UNDERSTANDING
GRAPHS

A. Look back at the graph on page 65. Then complete the description below.

The graph compares the world's most important and ¹_____ cities. Each

city gets a score in five areas as shown by the different colors. The green bar is business.

The ²_____ one is people. The blue one is ³_____. The

⁴_____ one is entertainment, and the pink one is ⁵_____.

ANALYZING

B. Use the graph on page 65 to answer these questions.

1. Which of these cities scores the highest for business?

a. New York City   b. London   c. Paris

2. In what area does Chicago score the highest?

a. business   b. people   c. media

3. How many cities have higher scores in politics than in entertainment?

a. none   b. one   c. two

CRITICAL THINKING Ranking Cities   Look at the graph on page 65 again. Of the 12 cities listed, which would you most like to live in? Choose three cities and rank them (1 = top choice). Then share your answers and reasons with a partner.

1. _____   2. _____   3. _____

VOCABULARY PRACTICE

DEFINITIONS **A.** Read the paragraph and match each word in **red** with its definition (1–5).

Times Square in New York City **attracts** about 50 million people every year, including many **international** tourists. It has a huge variety of entertainment **options** such as movie theaters, restaurants, and shopping. It is **especially** famous for its Broadway shows. City officials **predict** that Times Square will remain the most visited tourist spot in the United States for years to come.

▲ **Times Square, New York City**

1. _____ : choices
2. _____ : in particular
3. _____ : pulls; draws in
4. _____ : involving two or more countries
5. _____ : to say that something will happen in the future

WORDS IN CONTEXT **B.** Complete each sentence with the correct answer (a or b).

1. If you have **access** to something, you have _____ .
   a. a list of reasons to support it   b. a way to get or use it

2. An example of an **organization** is _____ .
   a. a teacher   b. the United Nations

3. Someone who is interested in **politics** is probably interested in _____ .
   a. how people choose their leaders   b. what websites people visit

4. If someone has **potential**, they have an ability that _____ be developed.
   a. can   b. cannot

5. Examples of **sources** of information might be _____ .
   a. questions and ideas   b. newspapers and websites

WORD PARTS **C.** The prefix *inter-* means "between" or "among" (e.g., *inter-* + *national* = **international**). Complete the sentences using the words in the box.

national	net	section

1. Many people today cannot imagine their lives without the **Inter**_____ .
2. Beijing has one of the world's busiest **inter**_____ airports.
3. New York's Times Square is located at the **inter**_____ of Broadway and Seventh Avenue.

BEFORE YOU READ

DEFINITIONS **A.** Read this paragraph and match each word in **bold** with its definition (1–3).

Every year, millions of people leave their country and **settle** in another one. In some cities, **immigrants** from a particular country live or shop in the same **neighborhood** (e.g., Chinatown in London).

1. _____ : an area in a city where people live

2. _____ : to go and live somewhere for a long time

3. _____ : people who have come to a foreign country to live

PREDICTING **B.** The reading passage discusses immigrants in São Paulo (Brazil) and Hamamatsu (Japan). What do you think is the connection between these two cities? Check your ideas as you read.

Residents celebrate a traditional Japanese festival in Liberdade, São Paulo, Brazil.

A TASTE OF TWO CITIES

A The city of São Paulo, Brazil, has hundreds of Japanese restaurants. A world away, in Hamamatsu, Japan, there are many places to buy and eat Brazilian food. Why is each country's food so **popular** in the other? The answer to this question dates back to the early 20th century.

B In 1908, people from Japan began moving to Brazil to work on coffee plantations.[1] Many of these Japanese immigrants (called *nikkei*) moved to São Paulo and settled in a neighborhood called Liberdade. Like many immigrants, they spoke their native language and prepared **traditional** foods from their home country. Over time, the *nikkei* opened many Japanese markets and restaurants in the Liberdade **district**. Today, this neighborhood has one of the largest Japanese **communities** outside of Japan. Restaurants sell ramen noodles and sushi on every corner. Also, each weekend, there is a large street market. Street sellers sell traditional Japanese **goods** and foods. The **event** is popular with both city residents and tourists.

C In the 1980s—three **generations** after the first *nikkei* settled in Brazil—a reverse migration began to take place. Over 300,000 Japanese-Brazilians moved to Japan, mainly to work in electronics and automobile factories. Many settled in Hamamatsu, a city on the east **coast** of Japan. Most Japanese-Brazilians spoke only their native language (Portuguese). They also missed the foods and culture of Brazil. Over time, a number of Brazilian restaurants and **stores** opened in Hamamatsu. Today, there is still a large Brazilian **population** in the city. All over Hamamatsu, food shops and restaurants sell traditional Brazilian foods, such as *pão de queijo* (a type of bread) and *feijoada* (a bean stew with beef and pork).

D Today, it's possible to eat excellent Japanese food in São Paulo and traditional Brazilian cuisine[2] in Hamamatsu. Whether traveling through Brazil or Japan, it's worth visiting these two cities to experience the tastes and cultures of their unique immigrant communities.

---

1 A **plantation** is a large farm on which crops such as coffee, tea, and sugar are grown.
2 **Cuisine** is a type of cooking (e.g., Brazilian cuisine, Italian cuisine).

A. Choose the best answer for each question.

PURPOSE

1. What is the main purpose of this passage?

    a. to discuss the challenges that immigrants face

    b. to explore the role of food in immigrant communities

    c. to compare immigration statistics in two different countries

DETAIL

2. The *nikkei* first came to Brazil ___ .

    a. to grow coffee

    b. as tourists

    c. to open restaurants

DETAIL

3. Which sentence about the street market in Liberdade is NOT true?

    a. It is a popular tourist attraction.

    b. It is open every day.

    c. You can try traditional Japanese dishes there.

REFERENCE

4. What does *Many* refer to in paragraph C?

    a. many factories

    b. many Japanese-Brazilians

    c. many generations

INFERENCE

5. The author's suggestion in the last sentence is directed to ___ .

    a. immigrants in general

    b. the *nikkei*

    c. tourists

EVALUATING STATEMENTS

B. Are the following statements true or false according to the reading passage, or is the information not given? Circle T (true), F (false), or NG (not given).

1. The *nikkei* opened Japanese schools in São Paulo.   **T F NG**

2. The main reason Japanese-Brazilians moved to Japan in the 1980s was to sell Brazilian goods.   **T F NG**

3. There is a large Brazilian street market in Hamamatsu every weekend.   **T F NG**

4. Many Japanese-Brazilians who moved to Japan in the 1980s and 1990s did not speak Japanese.   **T F NG**

5. *Feijoada* is a traditional Brazilian vegetarian dish.   **T F NG**

⌃ *Feijoada* is often called the national dish of Brazil.

Summarizing: Using a T-chart (1)

Instead of using a concept map to summarize the main ideas and supporting details from a text (see Unit 4A Reading Skill), you may choose to summarize information in a T-chart. A T-chart is especially useful when two things are discussed or compared, when a passage discusses the pros (advantages) and cons (disadvantages) of something, or when a passage provides the reasons for and against an argument.

ANALYZING   **A.** Look back at Reading B. Underline the main ideas and key details in the text.

SUMMARIZING   **B.** Complete the chart below with words or numbers from Reading B.

São Paulo, Brazil	Hamamatsu, Japan
In the past: • in 1908, many Japanese people began to move to Brazil to work on 1 _coffee_ plantations • immigrants (called *nikkei*) settled in 2 _liberdade_ (neighborhood) • spoke native language, ate foods from home country • opened Japanese 3 _market_ and restaurants *Today:* • very large Japanese community • Japanese foods (e.g., ramen and 4 _sushi_) widely available • Japanese street market each weekend; popular with locals and 5 _tourists_	*In the past:* • in the 6 _1980's_ , Japanese-Brazilians began to move to Japan (reverse migration) to work in electronics and car 7 _factories_ • immigrants settled in Hamamatsu (city) • spoke native language (8 _Portugese_), missed foods from home country • opened Brazilian restaurants and stores *Today:* • large Brazilian community • Brazilian foods (e.g., *pão de queijo*, a kind of 9 _bread_) widely available

CRITICAL THINKING Relating   Has your country's cuisine been influenced by foreign cuisines? How? Discuss with a partner and note your ideas. Include examples of dishes.

_____

_____

_____

COMPLETION **A.** Complete the paragraph with words from the box.

coast	district	goods	popular	stores	traditional

One of the most ¹___*popular*___ places for tourists to visit in Dubai is the Gold Souk, located in the Al Dhagaya ²___*district*___ on Dubai's northeastern ³___*coast*___. In contrast to the city's modern shopping malls, the souk is a ⁴___*traditional*___ Arabian market. It has over 300 ⁵___*stores*___ selling a wide range of gold jewelry and other ⁶___*goods*___. The total weight of all the gold in the souk is believed to be about 10 tons— about the same as two full-grown elephants!

A jewelry seller working in Dubai's Gold Souk

WORDS IN CONTEXT **B.** Complete each sentence with the correct answer (a or b).

1. The **population** of a country or an area is all the ___*a*___ in it.
   a. people   b. buildings

2. An example of an important **event** is a ___*b*___.
   a. school   b. sports competition

3. A **generation** is the period of time that it takes for children to ___*a*___.
   a. grow up and become adults   b. learn how to read

4. A **community** is a group of people who ___*b*___ a particular area.
   a. visit   b. live in

WORD FORMS **C.** We can add *-ation* to some verbs to form nouns (e.g., *generate* + *-ation* = **generation**). Use the noun form of these verbs to complete the sentences. One verb is extra.

communicate	generate	organize	populate

1. The total ___*population*___ of Brazil is over 211 million.
2. Listening is an important part of ___*communication*___.
3. A(n) ___*generation*___ ago, social media like Facebook and Twitter didn't exist.

> One Bryant Park (center) is among New York City's tallest buildings.

NEW YORK
SKYSCRAPER

BEFORE YOU WATCH

PREVIEWING   **A.** Read the information about One Bryant Park. Then discuss the questions (1–3) with a partner.

> **Name:** One Bryant Park (also known as the Bank of America Tower)
>
> **Year construction began:** 2004   **Year completed:** 2009
> **Height:** 288 meters   **Height including spire:** 366 meters
> **Number of floors:** 55   **Building cost:** $1 billion
> **Earth removed for foundation:** 198,000 cubic meters

1. How long did the building take to complete?
2. What part of the building do you think the spire is? How tall is the spire?
3. What part of the building do you think the foundation is?

PREDICTING   **B.** What do you think was challenging about building One Bryant Park? Discuss with a partner and note some ideas.

_____

_____

GIST **A.** Watch the video. Check (✓) the challenges of building a high-rise that the video discusses. Were any of your predictions in Before You Watch B mentioned in the video?

☐ a. digging the foundation   ☐ b. lifting materials up into the tower
☐ c. working in bad weather   ☐ d. driving big trucks through city traffic

COMPLETION **B.** Watch the video again. Circle the correct words to complete the sentences.

1. The crane operator is so high up that he is not able to *talk to the other workers* / *see what he is lifting*.

2. The workers have difficulty with the water tank because of its *large size* / *unusual shape*.

3. Michael Keen says that the city traffic "gets a little hairy at times." The word *hairy* probably means *dangerous* / *noisy*.

4. The building's spire is put together *on* / *above* the ground.

CRITICAL THINKING Evaluating Pros and Cons   What are some pros and cons of living in a city skyscraper like One Bryant Park? Discuss with a partner and complete this chart.

Pros	Cons

Do you remember the meanings of these words? Check (✓) the ones you know. Look back at the unit and review any words you're not sure of.

Reading A

☐ access*   ☐ attract   ☐ especially   ☐ international   ☐ option*
☐ organization   ☐ politics   ☐ potential*   ☐ predict*   ☐ source*

Reading B

☐ coast   ☐ community*   ☐ district   ☐ event   ☐ generation*
☐ goods   ☐ popular   ☐ population   ☐ store   ☐ traditional*

* Academic Word List

BACKYARD
DISCOVERIES

∧ A young explorer photographs a fern plant in a Canadian forest.

6A

DEFINITIONS **A.** Read the caption below. Match each word in **bold** with its definition (1–3).

1. _____ : living things

2. _____ : very small in size

3. _____ : the upper layer of the ground in which plants grow

PREDICTING **B.** Read paragraph A. Why do you think small organisms are important? Discuss with a partner. Then read the rest of the passage to check your ideas.

Around us there are millions of **tiny** plants, insects, fish, and other animals, but we often don't see them. Most of these **organisms** live in the **soil**, or (like the ones pictured) in the water. Some are only a millimeter in size.

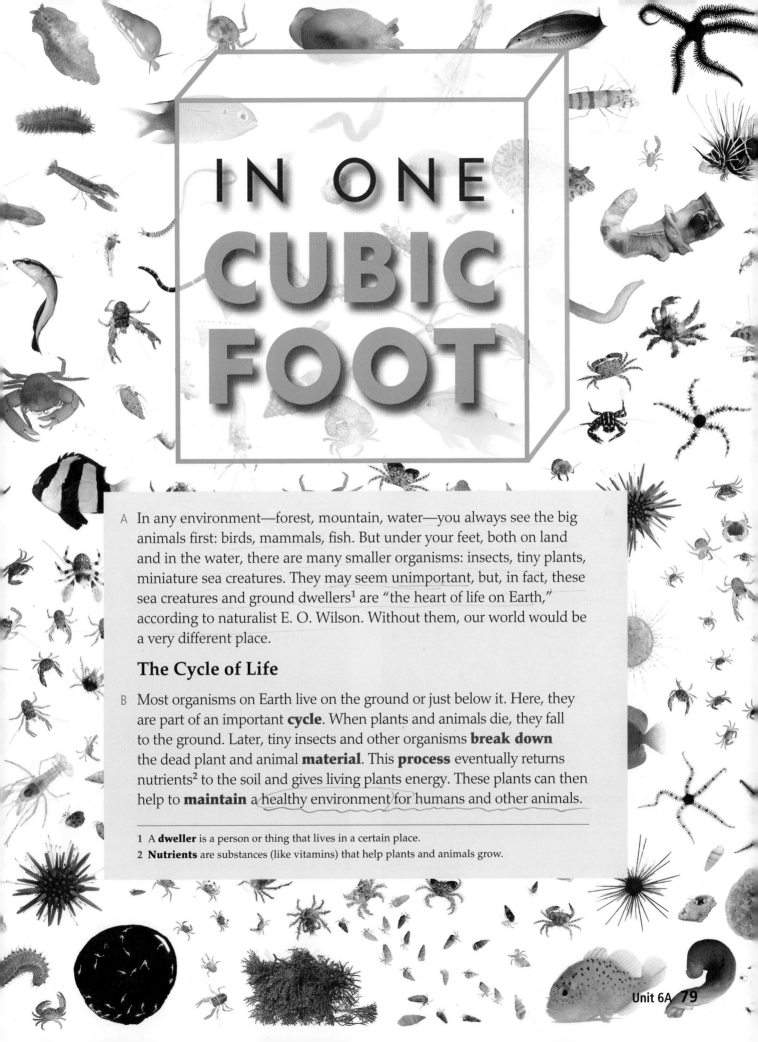

IN ONE CUBIC FOOT

A In any environment—forest, mountain, water—you always see the big animals first: birds, mammals, fish. But under your feet, both on land and in the water, there are many smaller organisms: insects, tiny plants, miniature sea creatures. They may seem unimportant, but, in fact, these sea creatures and ground dwellers[1] are "the heart of life on Earth," according to naturalist E. O. Wilson. Without them, our world would be a very different place.

The Cycle of Life

B Most organisms on Earth live on the ground or just below it. Here, they are part of an important **cycle**. When plants and animals die, they fall to the ground. Later, tiny insects and other organisms **break down** the dead plant and animal **material**. This **process** eventually returns nutrients[2] to the soil and gives living plants energy. These plants can then help to **maintain** a healthy environment for humans and other animals.

---

1 A **dweller** is a person or thing that lives in a certain place.
2 **Nutrients** are substances (like vitamins) that help plants and animals grow.

Discoveries in a Cube

C Despite their importance, **scientists** know very little about most ground organisms. To learn more, photographer David Liittschwager went to different places around the world, including a forest and a coral reef. In each place, he put a green 30-centimeter cube on the ground or in the water. Then he and his **team** counted and photographed the organisms that lived in or moved through the cube. Often they **discovered** hundreds of organisms, some only a millimeter in size. "It was like finding little gems,"[3] he says.

---

3 **Gems** are beautiful stones used in jewelry.

∨ Coral Reef
Moorea, French Polynesia
Here, Liittschwager photographed over 600 creatures in the cube. The team identified as many as possible, but it was difficult. Many of the animals they found were new **species**.

∨ Tropical Cloud Forest
Monteverde, Costa Rica
There are many different types of plants in this **region**. Almost 125 species that live here are found nowhere else on Earth.

A. Choose the best answer for each question.

GIST

1. What could be another title for this reading?

a. Tiny Organisms Are Everywhere
b. Saving Small Animals
c. The Life of a Photographer

VOCABULARY

2. In paragraph A, what does the word *miniature* mean?

a. very beautiful
b. very small
c. very important

DETAIL

3. Where do most organisms on Earth live?

a. in the sea
b. on land or in the soil
c. in the air

MAIN IDEA

4. Liittschwager and his team used the cube to _____ .

a. collect different species for further study
b. test the quality of the soil and water
c. count and photograph different organisms

INFERENCE

5. In paragraph C, why does Liittschwager call the organisms "little gems"?

a. He thinks they are valuable and precious.
b. They are very difficult for him to see.
c. The organisms look like small stones.

^ **David Liittschwager found this tiny baby octopus (1.1 cm across) in his coral reef sample.**

SHORT ANSWER

B. Write short answers for these questions. Use information from the reading passage and the photo captions.

1. What can plants help maintain for humans and animals?

healthy environment

2. Why was it difficult for Liittschwager's team to identify the creatures at the coral reef?

new species

3. Where did Liittschwager find over a hundred species that can't be found anywhere else?

Costa Rica

Understanding Sequence (1)—Processes

When you sequence events, you put them in the order in which they occur. Sequencing is important for gaining a deeper understanding of the relationship between events in a process. Some common words that can signal sequence are *first*, *after*, *then*, *later*, *next*, *once*, *when*, *as soon as*, and *finally*. A good way to show sequence is to list the events in a chain diagram.

IDENTIFYING **A.** Read paragraph B in Reading A again. Underline signal words that indicate a sequence.

SEQUENCING **B.** Put the life cycle events (a–f) in the correct order in the diagram below.

a. Plants and animals die.

b. Living plants get energy from the nutrients in the soil.

c. Plants help to support life for animals and humans.

d. Dead material is broken down.

e. Dead plants and animals fall to the ground.

f. Nutrients are returned to the soil.

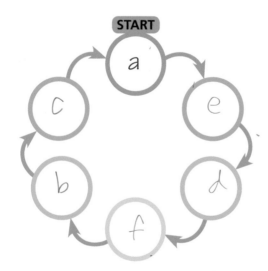

START

CRITICAL THINKING Applying Ideas   Imagine you are a member of Liittschwager's team. In which of the environments below would you place a cube? Why? Check (✓) three options and discuss with a partner.

☐ a city park   ☐ a riverbed   ☐ a cave

☐ a treetop   ☐ a backyard   ☐ a mountain

> Liittschwager photographed hundreds of species living in this 3,200-year-old giant sequoia tree.

COMPLETION   **A.** Circle the correct words to complete the information below.

One of the smallest animals in the world is a type of insect called a fairyfly. The male fairyfly of one [¹(species) / team] is only 0.17 millimeters in length—about the size of the period at the end of this sentence. Not much is known about the life [²(cycle) / species] of fairyflies. But we do know they don't live long—only between 2 and 11 days.

Fairyflies live mostly in rain forests. The ³**processes** / (**regions**) with the greatest number of species are in Australia, New Zealand, and South America. Recently, ⁴**materials** / (**scientists**) in Costa Rica ⁵(**discovered**) / **maintained** a new species of fairyfly called *Tinkerbella nana*.

∧ **The fairyfly is one of the world's smallest animals.**

WORDS IN CONTEXT   **B.** Complete each sentence with the correct answer (a or b).

1. A **process** refers to a _____ .
   (a.) series of events
   b. single event

2. If you **maintain** a healthy weight, it _____ .
   a. changes often
   (b.) doesn't change much

3. A **team** refers to _____ .
   a. just one person
   (b.) a group of people

4. Plant **material** would include _____ .
   a. rocks and stones
   (b.) grass and leaves

5. If you **break** something **down**, you _____ .
   (a.) separate it into smaller pieces
   b. give it away

COLLOCATIONS   **C. Break down** is one of many phrasal verbs formed using the verb *break*. Complete the definitions below using the prepositions in the box.

into	out of	up with

1. If you break __up with__ your boyfriend or girlfriend, your relationship with that person ends.
2. If a prisoner breaks __out of__ prison, they escape from it.
3. If someone breaks __into__ a building, they enter it by force.

BEFORE YOU READ

DISCUSSION **A.** Read this information. Then answer the questions below.

To learn about something (e.g., an animal or a plant), scientists must collect a lot of data. This can take a very long time. But now, regular people are helping scientists get important information more quickly. These "citizen scientists" take photos or interview other people. They then share their pictures and information with scientists on the Internet. Today, there are hundreds of citizen science projects—and anyone can join!

1. Who can be a citizen scientist?

2. What does a citizen scientist do? Why is this work important?

SKIMMING

Review this reading skill in Unit 1A

B. Read the introduction and the interview questions on the next page. Check (✓) the topics you think Gabby Salazar will discuss. Then read the interview to check your answers.

☐ a. different citizen science projects

☐ b. the problems with citizen science

☑ c. how to be a citizen scientist

National Geographic Explorer Gabby Salazar found this beautiful luna moth near her home in Pennsylvania, U.S.A.

WHAT'S IN YOUR NEIGHBORHOOD?

*Gabby Salazar takes photographs of **rare** species and teaches people about them. In this interview, she answers questions about her **experience** with citizen science.*

What was your first citizen science project?

A **Gabby Salazar:** It was over 10 years ago. One of my friends in Peru was very interested in birds. So we walked around with our cameras and notebooks for a day. We saw many different species, and we took photos of them. Later, we **posted** all our data on eBird.

What is eBird?

B **Gabby Salazar:** It's an Internet-based citizen science project at Cornell University in the United States. People around the world record information about birds they see. Today, eBird has over 590 million observations of more than 10,000 different bird species. Scientists use this data to answer important questions. For example: Where do certain birds live? How many are there?

How can a person become a citizen scientist?

C **Gabby Salazar:** It's easy. First, find a project that you like **online**. One of my favorites is iNaturalist, which studies animals and plants. Then, download the project's app[1] and use your phone to take pictures. For example, you can photograph different kinds of trees near your home or school. When you're done, **upload** your photos to iNaturalist. If you don't know the name of an animal or plant, other people can tell you. It's a great way to learn about your environment, and you also assist scientists with their **research**.

D If you can't take photos, you can still **contribute** to citizen science. For example, you can **take part** in a fun project called Wildwatch Kenya. Experts hide cameras in trees and other places. When an animal moves past, the camera takes a photo. Citizen scientists then **review** the **images** online and identify the animals they see.

THE LOST LADYBUG PROJECT

For years, scientists in North America thought the nine-spotted ladybug (pictured below) was extinct.[2] Then citizen scientist Peter Priolo photographed the insect in New York. He sent his photo to the Lost Ladybug Project, a site that is creating a map of different ladybug species. Now scientists know something important: The nine-spotted ladybug is rare, but not extinct.

---

1 An **app** (**application**) is a computer program for your phone or tablet.

2 If a species of animal or plant is **extinct**, it no longer exists.

A. Choose the best answer for each question.

PURPOSE

1. What is the purpose of this reading?

 a. to encourage people to take more photographs
 b. to describe somebody's experience with citizen science
 c. to answer important questions about certain bird species

DETAIL

2. Which of these statements about Gabby Salazar is <u>NOT</u> mentioned in the reading?

 a. She is a nature photographer.
 b. She is a citizen scientist.
 c. She is a motivational speaker.

REFERENCE

3. In the last sentence of paragraph D, what does *they* refer to?

 a. citizen scientists
 b. images
 c. animals

DETAIL

4. What did Peter Priolo send to the Lost Ladybug Project?

 a. an insect
 b. a photograph
 c. a map

INFERENCE

5. The nine-spotted ladybug _____ seen in New York.

 a. has never been
 b. can sometimes be
 c. is often

∧ **Salazar with a carnivorous pitcher plant, Mount Kinabalu, Malaysia**

EVALUATING STATEMENTS

B. Are the following statements true or false according to the reading passage, or is the information not given? Circle T (true), F (false), or NG (not given).

1. Salazar first became involved in citizen science through iNaturalist.   T   **F**   NG

2. More than 590 million bird observations have been uploaded to eBird.   **T**   F   NG

3. Salazar is paid for the photos that she posts online.   T   F   **NG**

4. To take part in the Wildwatch Kenya project, people need to travel to Africa.   T   **F**   NG

5. Salazar has won awards for her work.   T   F   **NG**

Understanding Sequence (2)—Instructions or Directions

Previously, you learned about signal words for a sequence of events (see Unit 6A Reading Skill). These signal words can also help you understand a sequence of steps for how to do something, or directions for how to get to a particular place. For example, notice the signal words in these instructions for how to photograph a sunset:

*First, get out there early to give yourself time to look around and find the best spot. **Next**, set up your camera. Try experimenting with different settings. **After** you have adjusted the settings, wait for the perfect moment and **then** take as many photos as you want. **Later**, you can develop the film or print out the pictures.*

SEQUENCING **A.** Reading B describes how to become a citizen scientist. Look back at paragraph C and number these steps in the correct order (1–4).

a. _3_ Take a photograph using your phone.
b. _4_ Upload the photo using the app.
c. _2_ Download the app to your phone.
d. _1_ Find an interesting citizen science project online.

COMPLETION **B.** Read about how to take part in a citizen science project called NestWatch. Then complete the notes with words from the paragraph.

NestWatch is a program in which people can watch and report on bird nesting sites. It's easy to get started. First, visit the website to take a short test. If you pass, you become a certified "NestWatcher." Next, read the website's tips on how to find a nest in your area. After you find a nest, visit it every three or four days and keep a record of what you see. Then upload your observations to the website. Researchers will use this information to track bird populations and how their nesting sites change over time.

How to Become a NestWatcher
1. Take a short test on the organization's 1 _website_.
2. Read the 2 _tips_ on the website for finding bird nests.
3. Find a 3 _nest_ in your area and 4 _visit_ it every 3–4 days.
4. Record your observations and 5 _upload_ them to the website.

CRITICAL THINKING Analyzing Information Find a citizen science project online. Note the following information about it and then describe the project to a partner.

Project name: _____

Purpose: _____

How you can take part: _____

_____

VOCABULARY PRACTICE

COMPLETION **A.** Complete the information with words from the box.

contribute	images	research	review	upload

Pl@ntNet is a citizen science project and an app that helps people identify plants using just their smartphones. It was developed by scientists from four French ¹ _research_ organizations. Users who know a lot about plants add photos and information to the database. Then, if someone wants to learn the name of a plant they see, they can download the app, take a photo of the plant, and ² _upload_ their photo to the database. The app will look for other plants in the database that look the same, and list the results. Finally, that user will need to ³ _review_ the results and confirm that their plant is one of the species from the list.

Currently, there are over 700,000 ⁴ _images_ in Pl@ntNet, and this number will continue to grow. "I think that users are quite proud to ⁵ _contribute_ to such a new collective knowledge," says Alexis Joly, one of the app's developers.

^ **An Alice sundew flower**

WORDS IN CONTEXT **B.** Complete each sentence with the correct answer (a or b).

1. When you **post** information on the Internet, you __b__.
   a. check it for accuracy
   b. make it available to other people

2. If you **take part** in an activity, you __b__.
   a. finish or complete it
   b. do it together with other people

3. Something that is **rare** is __b__.
   a. found in large numbers
   b. very unusual

4. If you have **experience** with a particular website, you __a__ used it before.
   a. have
   b. have not

5. If you are **online**, your computer __a__ connected to the Internet.
   a. is
   b. is not

COLLOCATIONS **C.** **Take part** is one of many collocations with the verb *take*. Complete the sentences using the words or phrases in the box. One option is extra.

a break	a photo	care	place

1. The conference will take _place_ in October.

2. It is everyone's responsibility to take _care_ of the environment.

3. The students had been studying for six hours, so they decided to take _a break_.

A young volunteer studies insects at a BioBlitz event in Hawai'i Volcanoes National Park.

BIOBLITZ

BEFORE YOU WATCH

PREVIEWING **A.** Read the information. The words in **bold** appear in the video. Match these words with their definitions below.

A BioBlitz is a citizen science event that focuses on finding and **classifying** as many species as possible in a specific area over one or two days. It brings together scientists and other **volunteers**, and it can take place anywhere—from a large national park to a small schoolyard. The goal is to create an **inventory** of all the species that live in an area, and to show that nature is all around us. In 2014, the National Geographic Society helped organize a BioBlitz in the Golden Gate National Recreation Area in the United States. Volunteers found a great **diversity** of plants and animals there, including freshwater sponges, rare butterflies and snakes, and even a mountain lion.

1. classify •   • a. someone who does work without being paid for it

2. volunteer •   • b. the state of being different or varied

3. inventory •   • c. to put things into groups according to type

4. diversity •   • d. a complete list of all the things that are in a place

DISCUSSION **B.** What are some problems that people might face during a BioBlitz event? Would you be interested in taking part in one? Discuss with a partner.

SEQUENCING **A.** Read the sentences below. Then watch the video and number these actions from the BioBlitz event in the order you see them (1–5).

a. ____ The volunteers work in the rain.

b. _2_ A group of people catch and identify animals from a river.

c. ____ The team leader announces how many species they found in the area.

d. ____ The volunteers use a white sheet to see animals in the dark.

e. ____ A young girl takes a close look at a frog.

MULTIPLE CHOICE **B.** Watch the video again. Choose the correct answer for each question.

1. In the video, what does John Francis say happens "in some cases"?

a. The BioBlitz takes longer than two days.

b. The team finds new species in the area.

2. What does John Johnson probably mean when he says, "Oh, nothing could be better"?

a. Some animals prefer to come out in rainy weather.

b. Even though it's raining, he's having a lot of fun exploring the area.

3. What is the purpose of the festival that is held after the BioBlitz?

a. to educate local people about the species in the area

b. to encourage people to sign up for the next BioBlitz event

4. How many species were discovered in this BioBlitz?

a. almost 2,000   b. over 2,000

CRITICAL THINKING Applying Ideas   Imagine you want to start your own citizen science project. What would it focus on? Note your ideas below and describe the project to a partner.

Project name: _____

Purpose: _____

How to take part: _____

_____

VOCABULARY REVIEW

Do you remember the meanings of these words? Check (✓) the ones you know. Look back at the unit and review any words you're not sure of.

Reading A

☐ break down   ☐ cycle*   ☐ discover   ☐ maintain*   ☐ material

☐ process*   ☐ region*   ☐ scientist   ☐ species   ☐ team*

Reading B

☐ contribute*   ☐ experience   ☐ image*   ☐ online   ☐ post

☐ rare   ☐ research*   ☐ review   ☐ take part   ☐ upload

* Academic Word List

Photo and Illustration Credits

Text Credits

Acknowledgments

The Authors and Publisher would like to thank the following teaching professionals for their valuable feedback during the development of the series.

Akiko Hagiwara, Tokyo University of Pharmacy and Life Sciences; **Albert Lehner**, University of Fukui; **Alexander Cameron**, Kyushu Sangyo University; **Amira Traish**, University of Sharjah; **Andrés López**, Colégio José Max León; **Andrew Gallacher**, Kyushu Sangyo University; **Angelica Hernandez**, Liceo San Agustin; **Angus Painter**, Fukuoka University; **Anouchka Rachelson**, Miami Dade College; **Ari Hayakawa**, Aoyama Gakuin University; **Atsuko Otsuki**, Senshu University; **Ayako Hisatsune**, Kanazawa Institute of Technology; **Bogdan Pavliy**, Toyama University of International Studies; **Braden Chase**, The Braden Chase Company; **Brian J. Damm**, Kanda Institute of Foreign Languages; **Carol Friend**, Mercer County Community College; **Catherine Yu**, CNC Language School; **Chad Godfrey**, Saitama Medical University; **Cheng-hao Weng**, SMIC Private School; **Chisako Nakamura**, Ryukoku University; **Chiyo Myojin**, Kochi University of Technology; **Chris Valvona**, Okinawa Christian College; **Claire DeFord**, Olympic College; **Davi Sukses**, Sutomo 1; **David Farnell**, Fukuoka University; **David Johnson**, Kyushu Sangyo University; **Debbie Sou**, Kwong Tai Middle School; **Devin Ferreira**, University of Central Florida; **Eden Kaiser**, Framingham State University; **Ellie Park**, CNC Language School; **Elvis Bartra García**, Corporación Educativa Continental; **Emiko Yamada**, Westgate Corporation; **Eri Tamura**, Ishikawa Prefectural University; **Fadwa Sleiman**, University of Sharjah; **Frank Gutsche**, Tohoku University; **Frank Lin**, Guangzhou Tufu Culture; **Gavin Young**, Iwate University; **Gerry Landers**, GA Tech Language Institute; **Ghada Ahmed**, University of Bahrain; **Grace Choi**, Grace English School; **Greg Bevan**, Fukuoka University; **Gregg McNabb**, Shizuoka Institute of Science and Technology; **Helen Roland**, Miami Dade College; **Hiroshi Ohashi**, Kyushu University; **Hiroyo Yoshida**, Toyo University; **Hojin Song**, GloLink Education; **Jackie Bae**, Plato Language School; **Jade Wong**, Belilios Public School; **James McCarron**, Chiba University; **Jane Kirsch**, INTO George Mason University; **Jenay Seymore**, Hong Ik University; **John Appleby**, Kanda Institute of Foreign Languages; **John Nevara**, Kagoshima University; **Jonathan Bronson**, Approach International Student Center; **Joseph Zhou**, UUabc; **Junjun Zhou**, Menaul School; **Kaori Yamamoto**; **Katarina Zorkic**, Rosemead College; **Keiko Miyagawa**, Meiji University; **Kevin Tang**, Ritsumeikan Asia Pacific University; **Kieran Julian**, Kanda Institute of Foreign Languages; **Kim Kawashima**, Olympic College; **Kyle Kumataka**, Ritsumeikan Asia Pacific University; **Kyosuke Shimamura**, Kurume University; **Lance Stilp**, Ritsumeikan Asia Pacific University; **Li Zhaoli**, Weifang No.7 Middle School; **Liza Armstrong**, University of Missouri; **Lucas Pignolet**, Ritsumeikan Asia Pacific University; **Luke Harrington**, Chiba University; **M. Lee**, KCC; **Maiko Berger**, Ritsumeikan Asia Pacific University; **Mandy Kan**, CNEC Christian College; **Mari Nakamura**, English Square; **Masako Kikukawa**, Doshisha University; **Matthew Fraser**, Westgate Corporation; **Mayuko Matsunuma**, Seijo University; **Michiko Imai**, Aichi University; **Mei-ho Chiu**, Soochow University; **Melissa Potts**, ELS Berkeley; **Monica Espinoza**, Torrance Adult School; **Ms. Manassara Riensumettharadol**, Kasetsart University; **My Uyen Tran**, Ho Chi Minh City University of Foreign Languages and Information Technology; **Narahiko Inoue**, Kyushu University; **Neil Witkin**, Kyushu Sangyo University; **Olesya Shatunova**, Kanagawa University; **Patricia Fiene**, Midwestern Career College; **Patricia Nation**, Miami Dade College; **Patrick John Johnston**, Ritsumeikan Asia Pacific University; **Paul Hansen**, Hokkaido University; **Paula Snyder**, University of Missouri-Columbia; **Reiko Kachi**, Aichi University / Chukyo University; **Robert Dykes**, Jin-ai University; **Rosanna Bird**, Approach International Student Center; **Ryo Takahira**, Kurume Fusetsu High School; **Samuel Taylor**, Kyushu Sangyo University; **Sandra Stein**, American University of Kuwait; **Sara Sulko**, University of Missouri; **Serena Lo**, Wong Shiu Chi Secondary School; **Shin Okada**, Osaka University; **Silvana Carlini**, Colégio Agostiniano Mendel; **Silvia Yafai**, ADVETI: Applied Tech High School; **Stella Millikan**, Fukuoka Women's University; **Summer Webb**, University of Colorado Boulder; **Susumu Hiramatsu**, Okayama University; **Suzanne Littlewood**, Zayed University; **Takako Kuwayama**, Kansai University; **Takashi Urabe**, Aoyama-Gakuin University; **Teo Kim**, OROMedu; **Tim Chambers**; **Toshiya Tanaka**, Kyushu University; **Trevor Holster**, Fukuoka University; **Wakako Takinami**, Tottori University; **Wayne Malcolm**, Fukui University of Technology; **Wendy Wish**, Valencia College; **Xingwu Chen**, Xueersi-TAL; **Yin Wang**, TAL Education Group; **Yohei Murayama**, Kagoshima University; **Yoko Sakurai**, Aichi University; **Yoko Sato**, Tokyo University of Agriculture and Technology; **Yoon-Ji Ahn**, Daks Education; **Yu-Lim Im**, Daks Education; **Yuriko Ueda**, Ryukoku University; **Yvonne Hodnett**, Australian College of Kuwait; **Yvonne Johnson**, UWCSEA Dover

GLOSSARY

These words are used in *Reading Explorer* to describe various reading and critical thinking skills.

Analyze   to study a text in detail, e.g., to identify key points, similarities, and differences

Apply   to think about how an idea might be useful in other ways, e.g., solutions to a problem

Classify   to arrange things in groups or categories, based on their characteristics

Evaluate   to examine different sides of an issue, e.g., reasons for and against something

Infer   to "read between the lines"—information the writer expresses indirectly

Interpret   to think about what a writer means by a certain phrase or expression

Justify   to give reasons for a personal opinion, belief, or decision

Rank   to put things in order based on criteria, e.g., size or importance

Reflect   to think deeply about what a writer is saying and how it compares with your own views

Relate   to consider how ideas in a text connect with your own personal experience

Scan   to look through a text to find particular words or information

Skim   to look at a text quickly to get an overall understanding of its main idea

Summarize   to give a brief statement of the main points of a text

Synthesize   to use information from more than one source to make a judgment or comparison

INDEX OF EXAM QUESTION TYPES

The activities in *Reading Explorer, Third Edition* provide comprehensive practice of several question types that feature in standardized tests such as TOEFL® and IELTS.

Common Question Types	IELTS	TOEFL®	Page(s)
Multiple choice (gist, main idea, detail, reference, inference, vocabulary, paraphrasing)	✓	✓	10, 16, 25, 30, 39, 44, 53, 58, 67, 72, 81, 86
Completion (notes, diagram, chart)	✓		54, 59, 62, 67, 73, 82
Completion (summary)	✓	✓	39
Short answer	✓		53, 81
Matching headings / information	✓		17, 25, 58
Categorizing (matching features)	✓	✓	10, 16
True / False / Not Given	✓		30, 44, 72, 86
Rhetorical purpose		✓	30, 53, 58, 72, 86

The following tips will help you become a more successful reader.

1 Preview the text

Before you start reading a text, it's important to have some idea of the overall topic. Look at the title, photos, captions, and any maps or infographics. Skim the text quickly, and scan for any key words before reading in detail (see pages 11 and 31).

2 Use vocabulary strategies

Here are some strategies to use if you find a word or phrase you're not sure of:

- **Look for definitions** of new words within the reading passage itself.
- **Identify the part of speech and use context** to guess the meaning of homonyms and new words.
- **Use a dictionary** if you need, but be careful to identify the correct definition.

3 Take notes

Note-taking helps you identify the main ideas and details within a text. It also helps you stay focused while reading. Try different ways of organizing your notes, and decide on a method that best suits you.

4 Infer information

Not everything is stated directly within a text. Use your own knowledge, and clues in the text, to make your own inferences and "read between the lines."

5 Make connections

As you read, look for words that help you understand how different ideas connect. For example:

- words that signal **reasons** (see page 45)
- words that indicate **sequence** (see pages 82 and 87)
- words that show degrees of **certainty**

6 Read critically

Ask yourself questions as you read a text. For example, if the author presents a point of view, are enough supporting reasons or examples provided? Is the evidence reliable? Does the author give a balanced argument? (see page 59)

7 Create a summary

Creating a summary is a great way to check your understanding of a text. It also makes it easier to remember the main points. You can summarize in different ways based on the type of text. For example:

- **timelines or chain diagrams** (see page 82)
- **T-charts** (see page 73)
- **Venn diagrams**
- **concept maps** (see page 54)
- **outline summaries**